Representatives and Roll Calls
A Computer Simulation of Voting
in the Eighty-eighth Congress

AN ADVANCED STUDY IN POLITICAL SCIENCE

Representatives
and Roll Calls

A Computer Simulation of Voting
in the Eighty-eighth Congress

Cleo H. Cherryholmes

Michigan State University

Michael J. Shapiro

University of Hawaii

THE BOBBS-MERRILL COMPANY, INC.
Indianapolis and New York

James A. Robinson
The Ohio State University
Consulting Editor

To Judy and Beppie

Preface

In 1901 A. Lawrence Lowell reported a pioneering study of legislative behavior. His investigation of party voting in the British Parliament and the United States Congress is notable as it was one of the first systematic studies of legislative bodies. Since that time, strides have been taken in the accumulation of empirical research findings in legislative behavior. As is true of many areas in political research, however, the literature has been characterized by discrete empirical studies that have not led to a general explanatory theory or set of theories. Generally, researchers have followed the strategy of selecting a few variables that seem important in the legislative process and have been content to determine the relationships among them.

Although several highly useful reviews of the literature have recently appeared (Meller, 1959 and 1965; Wahlke, 1962; Eulau and Hinckley, 1966), there have been few attempts to develop theoretical frameworks within which the welter of disparate findings could be systematically ordered. Meller (1965) noted that more empirical legislative studies had been completed between 1959 and 1965 than in the fifty years before 1959. The prospect of an explosion in research findings in the absence of more general integrating theories is unsettling if for no other reason than the problems of retrieving information it will pose.

Thus far, various systematic attempts to develop legislative behavior theory have produced only a partial yield. An investigation such as *The Legislative System* (1962) by Wahlke and his associates is a major theoretical contribution, because it carefully constructs and executes analyses of role systems within state legislatures. Their study begins with a set of theoretical constructs that are systematically employed in the collection and analysis of the data. But because roll-call votes are not a variable in this study, the role structures postulated and measured are not systematically related to legislative policy-making.

Theory development has also followed more inductive lines in which fewer theoretical constructs have guided the research. Many propositions concerning legislative behavior have achieved the kind of scientific status that can facilitate the development of theoretical models based upon them. The computer simulation model, whose structure and application is reported in this book, is an attempt at building a theory that utilizes the empirical findings on legislative behavior produced to date. The simulation model provides a framework within which propositions concerning the roll-call voting process in the U. S. House of Representatives can be combined to represent that process.

Clarkson and Simon (1960, p. 920) state, "The process of simulation involves constructing a theory, or model, of a system that prescribes the system's processes," and ". . . reproduces part or all of the output of a behaving system." The use of simulations in constructing political theory is receiving increasing attention (Guetzkow, 1962 and 1963; Hermann and Hermann, 1967; Klahr, 1966; Pool, Abelson, and Popkin, 1964 and 1965). Snyder (1963) notes four considerations "associated with this outburst of activity." First, many theoretical developments and problems cannot be examined with more traditional techniques because of the partial or complete absence of data. Second, there is a need for quick insights into problems that have no counterparts in our past experience. Third, computers have been developed that can rapidly explore the alternative implications of a theoretical model. Fourth, as models now range from a micro to a macro level focus, simulation provides a means of evaluating various aspects of macro level theory. These points, considered in the context of the present state of legislative behavior research, suggest the value of a computer simulation of roll-call voting.

Computer simulation is a dynamic modeling strategy which allows for the exploration of unanticipated outcomes. Experiments can be conducted that test the sensitivity of the simulation's output to various alternative formulations of the simulation model. In this manner, new propositions can be generated that can be tested later in the field. The development of a dynamic model allows processes to be represented and examined in ways not possible with other modes of theory representation. While much legislative research has been concerned with the static effects of party and constituency on roll-call voting, increasing attention is being devoted to institutional processes, such as the study of communication and influence patterns. A computer simulation model permits the effects of these processes to be simulated and evaluated.

Simulations also attract social scientists because they enable the researcher to assess the power of a theory in terms of its ability to predict a range of behavior with given numbers of variables or mechanisms. For our purposes, building an overall model that combines findings on roll-call behavior from more inductive studies and specifying which parts of the model are more or less corroborated, allows us to evaluate the model, and indirectly, the research upon which it is based. In addition, the model permits us to assess the power of the theory in a general sense as well as to evaluate its performance in specific issue areas and for particular types of representatives.

The first two chapters of our study are concerned with an overview of simulation strategies and of the state of legislative behavior research. In Chapters 3 and 4 we describe the construction of the computer simulation model in which verbal propositions are operationalized in the form of instructions for the computer. Chapters 5 and 6 present the performance of the simulation model on issues concerning the scope of the federal role, and Chapters 7 and 8 describe the model's performance on foreign affairs roll calls. In a concluding note, we assess all these experiences in terms of present and possible future contributions to legislative behavior theory.

Cleo H. Cherryholmes

Michael J. Shapiro

December 1968

Acknowledgments

It is always difficult to trace accurately the genesis and development of an idea. So it is with the research reported in the following pages even though the circumstances surrounding our work partially reduce the problem of attribution. The problem is reduced, in our case, because the work reported herein constituted two doctoral dissertations submitted to the Department of Political Science at Northwestern University. Our foremost debt of gratitude is enthusiastically paid to the Political Science faculty at Northwestern, and to their program of graduate training that helped us develop the skills and inclination that made our research venture possible. We are indebted to those who conceived the program and to those who carried it out in the classroom. Because the research was dependent on the computer, we are grateful for the generous assistance and consideration given to us by the Vogelback Computational Center.

Harold Guetzkow and Kenneth Janda deserve special thanks that extends far beyond their role as dissertation advisers. In addition to the support and encouragement rendered while the research was in progress, they helped to develop an intellectual environment that stimulated us to conceive of simulation methodology as a vehicle for integrating empirical findings into larger theoretical systems.

Finally we wish to thank our wives, Judy and Beppie, for their support and understanding of which great quantities were demanded and freely given.

Contents

Tables

Figures

Simulation

of Political Processes

As political science has evolved from its traditional concern of describing the institutions of government to a more theoretical enterprise, there has been a parallel attempt to develop and successfully apply more rigorous research methods. The application of quantitative research techniques to political phenomena has comprised what falls under the rubric of political behavior research. In this area, survey research has illuminated the process of voter decision-making, roll-call analysis has afforded insights into the determinants of representative decision-making, and a variety of modes of observation in laboratories and natural social settings have provided support for generalizations about "micro-politics" (Rokkan, 1962).

The legacy of behavioral analysis has consisted of insights into how and why individuals make certain social choices. At the macro, or system level, where the focus of political concern is on large policy-making aggregates such as nations, organizations, and legislatures, inquiry is still largely taxonomically rather than theoretically oriented. Exceptions have been the imaginative use of the laboratory to study the development of organizations (Guetzkow and Bowes, 1957) and

1

decision-making in town boards of finance (Barber, 1964), the use of factor analytic techniques to infer the dimensions of conflict processes within and between nations (Rummel, 1963; Tanter, 1964), and simulation techniques applied to the study of social and political processes in aggregates of varying sizes. Because simulation is the research method employed in our analysis of roll-call voting in the Eighty-eighth Congress, this chapter will analyze simulation techniques to provide a framework within which the results obtained from its application to congressional voting can be critically assessed.

SIMULATION TECHNIQUES: CLASSIFICATION AND DEFINITION

Numerous taxonomies of simulation, gaming, and related techniques have been preferred (Shubik, 1960; Dawson, 1962; Rapoport, 1964; Fattu, 1965; Cohen and Cyert, 1965). All of these classification schemes share a common interest in the interconnections of man and machine, particularly as they relate to the goals of the researcher. Perhaps the least controversial distinction is that between simulations and artificial intelligence. In the latter, no attempt is made to imitate real individuals as in the case of a simulation; rather, the concern is to imitate functions of individuals. The distinctions between games and simulations are more problematical. Generally, in a game, the behavior of the individuals participating is studied or influenced. In a simulation, (a man-computer as opposed to an all-computer) the individuals are inserted as convenient components (Shubik, 1960). Some prefer to distinguish games from simulations in terms of the degree to which the decision situations are structured, the game being the more highly structured situation (Abelson, 1968, p. 10).

There are two different perspectives concerning simulations in which human decision-makers are involved. From an operations research or problem oriented perspective, simulations are designed with a view toward optimizing the allocation of man-machine resources for a given task (Geisler, 1959; Ozkaptan and Gettig, 1963). When, on the other hand, theory building is of primary concern, humans are inserted where unprogrammed hypotheses and assumptions are needed to complement the programmed hypotheses and assumptions which do not, in themselves, constitute a complete enough deductive system to operate the simulation model (Guetzkow, 1959).

We are concerned with the computer or all-computer simulation.

Three essential features emerge from the numerous definitions which have been applied to computer simulations. Simulations involve (1) the symbolic or physical representation of some aspects of reality by (2) the construction of theories or models and (3) the operation and/ or manipulation of the theories or models.

Theories and Models

Because theories and models are essential aspects of social science simulations, an explication of the relationships between the two, in the context of constructing simulations, is in order. It is generally agreed that a scientific theory is a deductive system containing a set of initial hypotheses and a set of empirically testable generalizations. There is, however, far less agreement concerning models, both in terms of what they are, and how one should employ them.

The most prevalent dispute over the status of models is how synonymous are the terms "theory" and "model." At one extreme models are thought of as distinct from theories. Some maintain that a model is an approximation that can tolerate facts with which it is not in accord, while a theory is a conceptual system that aims at accurate description of the phenomena which it explains and must therefore be completely unimpeachable (Chapanis, 1961). This sort of position is predicated on a misconception of the nature of empirical science. Only the propositions that occur in pure mathematics or a content-free science can be falsified by the appearance of contrary cases. In the empirical sciences, various performance criteria are applied to theories, never the absolute true or false criterion.

At the other extreme is the view that models are isomorphic theories (Brodbeck, 1959). This position maintains that if the laws or propositions of one theory are structurally similar to those of another, one theory is a model of the other. This usage, while compatible with the cognitive orientation employed in modern empirical science, obscures useful distinctions among types of theories. As Kaplan has pointed out, theories all state that the subject matter has a given structure, but not all theories display that structure in themselves (1964, p. 265). His view is that the term "model" should refer only to those theories which suggest resemblances between the theoretical entities and the subject matter or data to which the theory refers.

From this perspective, the relationship between models and theories becomes clearer. Theories and models are analogues. The latter is the type of theory that is a working analogue in that it exhibits, in itself, the relationships among the entities for which it is an analogue. Modeling thus involves what Simon and Newell (1956) refer to as the psychological dimension of a theory, the content of a theory that is available to the researcher. The modeling strategy known as computer simulation attempts to render a theory's content available by articulating it in terms of a physical or mathematical model in which the instructions programmed for the computer correspond to the relationships between the theoretical entities prescribed by the verbal theory being modeled. That content can then be manipulated through changes in the programmed instructions.

Having assessed the definitional or formal relationship between theories and models, the question now is: What is the place of models in general, and simulation models in particular, in the scientific enterprise? As has been pointed out, models suggest themselves from the point of view of information processing considerations, for a theory in the form of a model can be manipulated or operated. This provides for both theory building and testing in that the model can be used to formulate hypotheses, which can be verified by laboratory and/or field experimentation and observation, and to validate or test hypotheses derived by others from their empirical investigations. The development of computer simulation models is a scientific strategy. It provides these theory building and testing capabilities in circumstances in which the subject matter under study presents complexities which preclude the use of direct mathematical formulation or other modeling strategies.

Modeling strategies possess advantages beyond those of the theory building and testing variety. Models can be used for prediction in ways that non-manipulable theories cannot because they can provide for the discovery of new generalizations about the data of observation. This feature is what Braithwaite has called "predictive novelty" (1962, pp. 228-229). The four types of predictive novelty which he discusses bear some consideration.

To begin with, consideration of the model may lead to the deduction of new propositions which were not represented in the original theory. These, in turn, could be employed to consider predictions not envisioned in the theory at the outset. In the second place, consideration of the model may reveal a new observable familiar property which, when combined with the other properties in the original propositions, would yield new propositions. One could then look for the property in the original theory, follow a parallel strategy, and deduce new generalizations. Both of these types of predictive novelty are not necessarily dependent on the employment of a model. The model may or may not aid in these new discoveries, for they are both possible in the context of working with the original theory.

It is the third and fourth types of predictive novelty which Braithwaite suggests as the major dividends of the modeling strategy. The third type results from considering the properties of the propositions of the model which might suggest new propositions which, when added to the original ones in the model, would provide for new generalizations. Moving then to the theory, one could add the new hypotheses and obtain an extended theory with new empirically testable generalizations.

The fourth type of predictive novelty results from the extension of the number of observable properties such that their combination with the other properties would yield new initial propositions which would, in turn, produce new generalizations about the theoretical terms of the model. Again, a parallel procedure would be suggested for the original theory with the result that the theory would be extended to include not only new hypotheses, but hypotheses containing new theoretical terms. In these last two types of predictive novelty, the model serves to point in the direction of the extension of the theory, an occurrence not as likely, working in the context of the original theory. The exploitation of all these possible advantages which can accrue from the modeling strategy is perhaps most feasible in the case of computer simulation models which allow for simultaneous manipulation of an extremely large number of mechanisms.

Before turning to a discussion of computer simulations, however, one more aspect of the model-theory relationship should be considered. Not all models are designed for the purposes of theory building and testing. Berger, Cohen, Snell, and Zelditch (1962), for example, distinguish between explicational, representational, and theoretical-construct models. As these terms suggest, the first two types of models are used to explicate and represent theories, the role of the former being one of rendering precise one or more of the basic concepts of a theory, and the latter one of representing precisely and simply a particular type of phenomena described in a theory. The theoretical-construct model is the type that relates to our foregoing discussion of the advantages of the modeling strategy. In this type, the goal is one of developing a general explanatory theory to render meaningful a given subject matter.

COMPUTER SIMULATIONS: THEORY BUILDING AND MANIPULATION

While susceptibility to manipulation[1] is one of the prime recommendations of the modeling strategy for theory building and testing, there is a sense in which manipulation and theory building are incompatible. As was mentioned, theories in the empirical sciences are not evaluated on the basis of an absolute true or false criterion. As Milton Munitz puts it, "Theories are apt or fitting but they are not as such true, where truth is taken to mean 'correspondence of symbol and existence' " (1957, p. 42). The criteria for evaluating whether theories are apt or fitting center around the functions for which theories are employed. Among other things, theories function as "systematically unifying schema for qualitatively diverse subject matter" (Munitz, 1957, p. 42). The criterion for evaluating this function has been expressed in various ways. One recent formulation refers to the "organizing efficiency" of a theory. This is defined as the ratio of the number of cases or the range of the data to which the theory can be applied to the number of relevant variables distinguished by the theory to be evaluated (Deutsch, Singer, and Smith, 1965).

The fundamental strain between the theory building and manipulation functions of modeling should be evident. In order to maximize manipulation potential, as many variables or mechanisms as possible are built into a model. The organizing efficiency or power of the theory,[2] however, would vary inversely with the number of variables included to represent those elements of the subject matter considered significant. In the case of computer simulation models, this antinomy is manifested in the two fundamentally different purposes for which simulation models are constructed. These are the theory building and testing functions and the problem solving functions distinguished on page 2. Because most computer simulations are designed with both

---

[1] Susceptibility to manipulation is defined in terms of the number of mechanisms used to represent the theoretical relationships.

[2] For the remainder of the discussion efficiency and power will be equivalent terms to denote the organizing ability criterion of a theory.

manipulation and theoretical development in mind, simulation models can be characterized by their position on a continuum with maximum manipulative potential at one end, and maximum organizing power or efficiency at the other.

Considering, first of all, simulations of cognitive processes, we find simulation models of human problem solving near the manipulation end of the continuum. Attempts at simulating the cognitive processes involved when individuals solve problems in logic, for example, require the inclusion of a large number of variables or mechanisms because of the complexity of the process involved (Newell, Shaw, and Simon, 1958; Newell and Simon, 1963). Other cognitive process simulations at this end of the continuum include Feldman's computer models of binary choice experiments. Feldman (1963) attempts to develop models of the pattern of choices each subject makes when attempting to predict the frequency of occurrence of two events, and Hunt and Hovland's (1961) computer models of human concept formation in which such mechanisms as recognition, internal memory, answer developing, and answer checking are included. The proliferation of mechanisms stems, in Feldman's models, from the attempts to develop separate models for each subject. In Hunt and Hovland's models the proliferation originates from the complexity of the concept formation process as they conceptualize it.

In the middle range of the continuum we encounter Feigenbaum's model of verbal learning behavior (1963) and Loehlin's model of personality (1963 and 1965). In the case of Feigenbaum's model, the complexity of the process necessitates the inclusion of several mechanisms, but a degree of parsimony is achieved by keeping the number of processes involved at a minimum and focusing on an abstract individual rather than on particular subjects. Thus by reducing verbal learning behavior to two sub-processes, learning and performing, Feigenbaum achieves some organizing efficiency or power despite the complexity of the process being modeled.

Loehlin also obtained some organizing power in his computer model of personality by including only three main sub-processes: recognition, emotional reaction, and action preparation. The power of his theoretical formulation was somewhat vitiated, however, by the need to include several mechanisms within each sub-process in order to attain his goal of assessing the implications of confrontations between different personality types.

Among those cognitive process simulation models occupying the organizing power end of the continuum are those concerned with belief or perceptual systems. In these, an attempt is made to develop and test powerful theories to explain such aspects of belief systems as "hot" or affective cognition (Abelson, 1963), neurosis (Colby, 1963; Colby and Gilbert, 1964), and resistance to attitude change(Abelson and Carroll, 1965). In the case of the computer model of a neurotic belief system, organizing power is obtained by grouping the mechanisms involved within two basic "action postulates." These strive to express beliefs in belief complexes and attempt to maintain retention of beliefs evaluated as dangerous. Abelson and Carroll, in studying the problem of resistance to attitude change, attain organizing power by adducing the mechanisms in their simulation model from an extension of the cognitive balance theory (Abelson and Rosenberg, 1958; Abelson, 1959; Rosenberg and Abelson, 1960; Abelson, 1963).

Simulation models of processes in formal organizations are also susceptible to evaluation on the basis of our organizing power-manipulation continuum. Occupying the manipulation end of the continuum are operations research-type simulations in which very little substantive theory is embodied. Perhaps the most extreme example of this type is Ritti and Fair's simulation of a factory system (1965). Regarding their program as a "computational algorithm" rather than a theoretical model, they operate their simulate by manipulating the values of all their variables which are included in one large covariance matrix.

Mainly theoretical, but near the manipulation end of the continuum, are those simulations of organizations classified by Cohen and Cyert as descriptive (1965). These include Cyert, March, and Moore's simulation of department store buying (Cyert and March, 1963, pp. 128–148), and Clarkson's simulation of the portfolio selection process (1962). In the former are included mechanisms to represent, in some detail, the process exhibited by a department store buyer when selecting and pricing merchandise. The goal is the systematic exploration of the behavior patterns produced by the model. In the latter, a model of the behavior of a trust investment officer choosing investment policies is developed with the inclusion of three sub-processes: memory, search and selection, and rule evaluation. While this economy of processes is suggestive of theoretical organizing power, the fact that all the mechanisms within these processes represent the decision-making behavior of one trust investor suggests the opposite.

At the middle range of the continuum for organizational simulations are Cohen's simulation of the shoe, leather, hide sequence (1960), Balderston and Hoggat's simulation of the West Coast lumber industry (1962), and Cohen, Cyert, March, and Solberg's simulation of price and output determination in oligopoly firms (Cyert and March, 1963, pp. 149–182). In all of these a large number of mechanisms are included for the purposes of manipulation, but a degree of organizing power is attained in the model of Cohen, Cyert, March, and Solberg because of its applicability to several firms, and in the Cohen and Balderston and Hoggat models by virtue of their degree of abstraction from the actual subject matter.

Moving to the organizing power end of the continuum for organization simulation models we find that Bonini's computer model of information and decision systems in the firm qualifies for placement here despite its focus on one organization (1963). Basing his model upon propositions dealing with pressure and organizational slack, Bonini constructs the model around individuals at three levels in the firm. He maintains the same type of specifications for each level. The behavior of each individual is specified as a function of the behavior of the individuals at the other levels and the amount of past and present information available. These mechanisms are involved in the two basic processes: pressure resulting from information of the accounting type and the contagion of pressure down through the organization. Thus, with a minimum of organizing concepts, Bonini models the decision-making behavior of the individuals in the key decision centers of the firm.

Turning finally to simulations of social processes, we find most of these simulation models clustering toward the organizing power end of the continuum. Alone at the manipulation end is Coleman's simulation of sociometric ratings in large groups (1961). This status is accorded his simulation model because it is primarily aimed at variable manipulation and, as such, lacks organizing concepts. His purpose was not to develop a theoretical model, but to construct a tool to simplify a calculation process.

In the middle range of the continuum of social process simulations is Orcutt, Greenberger, Korbel, and Rivlin's simulation model of the United States socioeconomic system (1961). In this highly complex model are included mechanisms for decision-making units such as families, firms, banks, and markets. These mechanisms are combined in a dynamic model by utilizing outputs from one group of mechanisms as inputs for another. Although an extremely large number of mechanisms are included in the model, theoretical organizing power is obtained by building on the basis of theoretical generalization at the micro level and combining the aggregate data and relationships to complete the overall model.

Grouped at the organizing power end of the continuum are two types of social process simulations; those concerned with interactions in small groups, and those concerned with the processes involved in voting decisions. Among the small group interaction models are Hare's simulation of the perceptions of new group members based upon the theories of value homophily and social interaction (1961), the Gullahorn's simulation models of interpersonal interaction, based upon the theories of George Homans (1963 and 1965), and Coe's simulation of aggressive behavior based upon the theories of Hamblin and others (1964). In each of these cases, models of interpersonal interaction are constructed and operated with relatively few mechanisms involved in order to investigate the power of the theory being modeled.

The simulation models of voting systems include McPhee's simulation model of a Wisconsin primary (1961 and 1963), Coleman and Waldorf's simulation model of voting in Baltimore in the 1960 presidential election (1962), Pool, Abelson, and Popkin's simulations of the 1960 and 1964 presidential elections (1964 and 1965), and Abelson and Bernstein's simulation model of fluoridation referenda (1963). Three of these models begin at the individual level and include both predisposition and discussion or interaction processes. McPhee's model begins with a distribution of partisanship preferences, moves to a confrontation of these with the issues and/or candidates in the campaign, and continues into a discussion process. Coleman and Waldorf's model also begins with initial attitudes toward candidates and continues with a mediation of those attitudes through comparison with issues and attitudes of one's associates. Abelson and Bernstein's model similarly begins with attitudes toward the issues and various arguments on either side, and exposes each individual to both mass media and discussion channels. In all three, the processes are based upon social-psychological theories of the ways in which attitudes are influenced.

Pool, Abelson, and Popkin's presidential election simulations differ from the above three in that no processes are involved. They construct synthetic states on the basis of the distribution of voting types in each, and then plug each state's totals into equations representing their theoretical formulations of the factors determinative of the voting preferences of each type. The equations which proved successful for the 1960 election were formulated on the basis of propositions about the effects of "cross-pressure" derived from the voting studies of Lazarsfeld and his associates (Lazarsfeld, Berelson, and Gaudet, 1948; Lazarsfeld, Berelson, and McPhee, 1954). The successful equations employed for the 1964 election were based upon the ways in which each voting type could be expected to react to the three major issues in the campaign. It is evident that these simulation models are far more powerful than the three already discussed, but it is equally evident that, because of the paucity of mechanisms and lack of processes included, these models cannot be employed to illuminate the dynamics of voter decision-making. The models were, in fact, designed for a limited function: the prognostication of the election outcomes in each state.

SIMULATION AND THE LOGIC OF DISCOVERY

The use of simulation in the social sciences requires, in some cases, a sacrifice of theory power for theory manipulation on the part of the researcher. As has been pointed out, the character of social research is such that a large amount of data and a relatively large number of variables are necessities in the theory building process (Herniter, 1965). This is true in particular when the subject matter is a large aggregate such as an electorate or a legislature. The simulation strategy replaces, for the researcher, the more powerful direct mathematical formulation of the theory, but provides an analogue of the theory that can be operated or manipulated to consider, successively, alternative formulations of the theory and alternative weights for the variables and constants in the propositions of the theory.

From the point of view of the logic of discovery, the simulation strategy includes a combination of inductive and deductive approaches to theory building. The process of discovery begins with both theory and data and ends, hopefully, with a theory that is more "apt or fitting" than that with which the inquiry was begun. The inquiry proceeds, in fact, in the manner prescribed by Aristotle as suitable for all scientific inquiry. In his *Posterior Analytics* he asserts that in the pursuit of scientific knowledge one begins with both consideration of the observations conducted thus far and rudimentary first principles (the underived propositions of a theory). One employs dialectical reasoning to test the compatibility of these first principles with the data of observation, formulates new first principles, continues the dialectical reasoning, and so on until the combination of intuition and observation results in the first principles that are the proper ones for the subject matter (Tredennick, trans., 1960).

Aside from Aristotle's commitment to the status of the first principles of an empirical science (he regarded the end of inquiry as coincident with the discovery of the true first principles), the philosopher's account of the logic of discovery parallels many accounts of the use of simulation models in theory development. Consider, for example, the following:

A basic practice of the research worker is to analyze past behavior of the system under study by considering historical data. From this analysis he may acquire enough background to build a tentative mathematical model. This is tested with actual data to see whether the obtained data are reasonable enough. The model, then, can be modified accordingly. This modified model needs to be tested again until a simulation close enough to reality results (Chorufas, 1964, pp. 16–17).

One aspect of the process of scientific discovery to which both Aristotle and Chorufas allude deserves more than perfunctory consideration. This is the relationship between the theory or simulation model and reality. At a general or informal level, a simulation model has been described as touching upon reality in four ways: (1) the model bears upon the real world through our attempts to pattern the decision rules upon received knowledge from the empirical work in various disciplines, (2) the completed model is a description of real world phenomena, (3) the model is used to formulate hypotheses about the real world, (4) the model can be used to validate or test hypotheses derived by others from the real world (Bonini, 1963).

But the philosophical problems which attend the ascription of reality to any observable situation require a more critical formulation of the relationships as in the following:

Formally, a simulation model is an operator which generates a set of variable X, given a set of variables Y, such that (a) the set of variables X and Y represent characteristics of the referent situation, (b) the set of variables X is indistinguishable with respect to an explicit criterion from the corresponding characteristics of the referent situation, and (c) the operator itself represents the causal processes relating the characteristics of the referent situation (Starbuck, 1961, p. 191).

The term "referent situation" helps us to distinguish the situation that we are trying to create from the situation that we are trying to apprehend without involving us in an ontological commitment which we cannot justify. We create a situation with causal rules for its operation based upon our hypotheses concerning those causal rules which explain the operation of the referent situation. From the point of view of the logic of discovery we consider not how real the simulation model is but how well it performs in terms of rendering more explicable the referent situation or subject matter with which we are concerned.

SIMULATION OF POLITICAL PROCESSES

At the outset it was asserted that the simulation strategy is one that suggests itself as a quantitative research technique for macro level political analysis. The concept of a system may lend itself to the assessment of this assertion. While there are competing notions as to what constitutes a social or political system, it is generally agreed that a system includes a structure or set of relatively stable units with given attributes (both static and relational) and processes which involve interchanges between the basic units, altering, in some instances, the attributes of those units.

Thus, a computer simulation of a political process involves the delimiting of the system within which the process takes place by choosing theoretical terms that will represent those structural properties (units and attributes of units) thought to be essential to the process. As has been suggested, the number of units and attributes chosen will have implications for both the organizing power of the theory being modeled and the manipulative potential of that theory.

The process itself is represented by the computer program, which as a theory of a political process (Browning, 1962), specifies or prescribes the dynamics of the relationships among the units of the structure as the system receives various inputs. When the political process being modeled produces observable outputs, the outputs of the simulation can be compared with those of the referent system to validate the simulation model. The simulation of political processes enables us to go beyond political behavior research by providing a method for aggregating propositions about micro political phenomena in a dynamic model in which outputs of various micro level relationships become inputs that initiate the operation of other relationships; the result is theoretical development at the macro political level.

The simulation of roll-call voting in the Eighty-eighth session of the U.S. House of Representatives, bears some resemblance to the voting simulations of the primary election (McPhee, 1961 and 1963) and the fluoridation referenda (Abelson and Bernstein, 1963) inasmuch as our model has two phases, cognition and communication. Within these two phases are contained the processes and mechanisms with which we have attempted to build a theoretical overview of legislative voting behavior.

We have attempted to do more than predict (or, more accurately, postdict) voting outcomes as in the case of Pool, Abelson, and Popkin's election simulations. Our model is constructed with a view toward identifying the processes and determinants of legislative voting decisions as well as approximating the results of those decisions. To determine the extent to which we approximate outcomes, our simulated voting is compared with the actual voting on the same bills. The identification of processes and determinants requires more than inference on the basis of this matching of outcomes. This aspect of our investigation is conducted by constructing alternative formulations of our simulation model to determine the extent to which the processes and determinants included in the original model are significantly involved in producing simulated voting outcomes that match the actual ones.

In constructing our model we have grouped propositions concerning the determinants of roll-call voting behavior into predisposition and communication processes in order to develop a theoretical model that contains the significant aspects of the legislative processes with a minimum of conceptual apparati. In the predisposition phase of our model are propositions drawn from social-psychological studies of attitude formation in general and legislative research in particular to provide a theory of the determinants of the voting predispositions that emerge from the cognitions of representatives confronted with legislation. The communication phase contains propositions drawn from legislative research concerning the likelihood of communicative interaction between various types of legislators, and propositions drawn from face-to-face group research concerning the attitude change resulting from interactions between individuals with different predispositions or attitudinal postures.

At a general level, then, our simulation model can be assessed in terms of its conceptual structure. Our attempt is to utilize two basic processes to organize the propositions of our theory efficiently. At another more specific level, however, our concern is with exploiting the manipulation potential of the computer model in order to determine the extent to which the conceptual structure explains the process or referent situation, and to investigate the significance of the various components of the conceptual structure in terms of their contributions to the explanatory capacity of the model as a whole. The process of investigation at this level is subsumed under the concept of validation. Hermann (1965) has noted five criteria for validating a simulation model: (1) internal validity, (2) face validity, (3) event validity, (4) variable-parameter validity, and (5) hypothesis validity. In varying degrees, each of these approaches will be utilized to appraise our computer model. This utilization of different methods of evaluation is based on the notion that each validity strategy by itself may overlook non-representative aspects of the model (Campbell and Fiske, 1959).

In operating a simulation, relationships and parameters may be adjusted until a "best fit" is produced. Such a best fit may be a "lucky guess" and not be theoretically sound or be representative of other critical features of the referent situation. For example, Pool, Abelson, and Popkin (1965, pp. 80–81) achieved a best fit in their simulation of the 1960 presidential election that was not theoretically satisfying in relation to other theories and data on election behavior. Thus a simple matching of our simulated votes may be misleading; simulation output must be viewed within the total context of legislative theory and research.

By systematically employing different approaches to simulation validity it should be possible to evaluate more adequately simulation output in relation to the research literature than by the use of any one criterion. The internal validity of the simulation model will be assessed by noting variation among identical runs: "The smaller the between-run variance, the greater the internal validity is assumed to be" (Hermann, 1965, p. 4). The issue of face validity may be more applicable to all-man or man-computer simulations where rigorous statistical tests are more difficult to apply, but in the present case face validity was partially dealt with by designing the model on the basis of legislative theory and research.

Event, variable-parameter, and hypothesis validity may represent rather objective and rigorous comparisons of the simulate with the referent system. Event validity, as applied to the simulation model, has a limited meaning. The occurrence of the event—the roll call—is a foregone conclusion because without a vote input no action would occur in the simulation. The roll-call result, however, may be treated as the event to be compared across the simulated and reference system. At a macro level, then, whether a vote was passed or defeated in the simulation and in the actual House vote, along with a comparison of the yeas and nays, will constitute our use of event validity.

Variable-parameter validity represents a more sensitive appraisal of a simulation model. As already noted, one advantage of simulation is that it permits the model to be manipulated. By systematically changing the coding on bills processed by the simulation model, it is possible to determine whether the variables that legislative research associates with a given set of roll calls are associated with a similar set of roll calls in the simulation. For example, Turner (1951) has convincingly demonstrated that party is the most important single determinant of congressional voting. If this proposition holds for our simulation model, it will perform better on roll-call votes coded on "just party" than on any alternative single coding. Another example of a variable-parameter test would be to investigate the roll calls on which just party and "just memory" coding resulted in the closest correspondence to actual votes.[3] MacRae (1956) illustrated the existence of two dimensions of party loyalty: loyalty to the organization and loyalty to the ideology. If roll calls are "miscoded," the representativeness of simulation output will be reduced. Thus, if votes commanding loyalty to the organization are coded as ideological issues, the model will be demonstrably less representative of congressional behavior than if these votes had been coded as organization roll calls. By alternatively isolating variables and parameters of legislative voting those aspects of the model producing and reducing simulate-referent agreement may be identified.

Hypothesis validity will be used to evaluate the model by applying propositions derived from legislative research to simulation behavior. One such hypothesis to be investigated is the relative cohesion of the majority and minority parties. If the majority party is less fluid

[3] The role played by coding of bills in the setting of simulation parameters will be explicated in Chapters 3, 5, and 7.

than the minority, as we have been led to expect (Truman, 1959), it should be less subject to chance factors and, therefore, be more predictable. By this indirect route we are led to the expectation that the simulation model will perform with greater accuracy for the votes of majority members than for the minority, by the simple fact that they are more predictable. Other hypotheses, many of them concerning the groups that are more predictable, will also be used to evaluate the simulation model's performance.

Finally to demonstrate the interplay of inductive and deductive theory building strategies, which attend the use of simulation modeling, we employ different testing sequences in the application of the model to specific roll calls. In simulating roll calls dealing with the federal role (Chapters 5 and 6), we begin with our best fit model and indicate the relative significance of various of its components by simulating the same roll calls with stripped down versions of the original model. In simulating roll calls dealing with foreign policy (Chapters 7 and 8), we begin with a "basic coding" model and systematically add components to improve the model's performance.

Legislative Behavior Research: The Basis for a Computer Model

A simulation of an event, process, or institution is highly dependent upon extant theory. The form and operation of our model of roll-call voting in the U.S. House is based upon empirical legislative research. Specifically, research which has been selected for review is that which has either used roll-call votes as the dependent variable, or which has focused on variables or processes that seem closely related to roll-call voting.

One group of congressional roll-call studies relate legislative voting decisions to discrete, explanatory variables. The variables most commonly investigated include: (1) party affiliation, (2) constituency type, (3) section or region, and (4) individual characteristics. MacRae has noted:

> Some representatives may vote together because of the influence of their associates; but others may vote together without there having been interaction on the subject, simply because of similarity in the constituencies they represent, or the similarity of their personal backgrounds (1954, p. 192).

The following discussion of the research literature will focus partially on research of this latter kind.

A second group of legislative voting studies has examined the social system of legislatures. Aspects of legislative behavior that have been investigated are, among others: (1) communication, and (2) norms. To the extent that these processes and expectations seem related to roll-call behavior they will be discussed and used in the development of the computer model. The primary, but not exclusive, criterion employed in identifying legislative research upon which the model is based is the use of roll-call votes as the dependent variable.

A general strategy of a social and/or political simulation is:

> . . . to link together known microprocesses in a particular structural configuration, in order to examine consequences at the level of the system (Coleman, 1963, p. 1054).

Legislative research findings that relate variables and processes to roll-call behavior constitute the microprocesses that will be used in constructing a model of legislative voting; the roll-call votes represent "consequences at the level of the system." The computer program is a structural and procedural analogue of voting in a legislative body— the U.S. House of Representatives.

This chapter will survey research findings relating roll-call voting to: (1) party, (2) constituency, (3) region, and (4) individual characteristics. Because of the relevance to legislative decision-making, social features of legislative bodies to be discussed include: (1) communication and (2) legislative norms. Research findings do not usually lend themselves to neat taxonomies; it will become clear as the discussion proceeds that most of the research cannot be placed entirely within any one of the categories. It is encouraging, however, that overlap does not exist merely in terms of research design but in the more important area of substantive conclusions. For example, some legislative norms help explain why certain communication patterns exist, which in turn contributes to an explanation of particular aspects of roll-call voting. In an attempt to clarify the findings in each category and to outline the areas of convergence among them, summary propositions will be stated at the end of each section. In most cases these propositions have been suggested by the foregoing discussion.

PARTY AFFILIATION AND ROLL-CALL BEHAVIOR

Many acknowledge the political party of a representative to be the single most important factor in legislative voting (Turner, 1951 and 1951a; Froman, 1963; Havens, 1964; Marwell, 1967). Consequently party has been studied more frequently than other independent variables in analyzing legislative roll-call behavior:

Party pressure seems to be more effective than any other pressure on congressional voting, and is discernible on nearly nine-tenths of roll calls examined (Turner, 1951, p. 23).

Contrary to popular impression, the parties usually maintain their ranks on congressional votes, including those of headline significance, with sufficient solidarity so that voters may distinguish between two points of view (Turner, 1951, p. 145).

Turner posed the question of party loyalty in a statistical framework: Does roll-call variance *between* the parties significantly exceed roll-call variance *within* the parties? In looking at four sessions of Congress from 1921 to 1944 (pp. 14, 15), Turner used Lowell's test of a party vote (although the percent defining a party vote was reduced from 90 to 80 of each party voting in opposition to the other party), Rice's Index of Party Likeness (Rice, 1925), and the chi-square test of significance. Seventeen percent of the roll calls met the party vote criterion (p. 24); on the basis of the chi-square analysis, 407 of 455 roll calls exhibited party influence at the .05 level of significance (p. 31). The strength of party influence across different issues was analyzed by the Index of Party Likeness. Turner found sharp, consistent party cleavage on tariff, government action, social and labor, and farm issues. Patronage, control of the house, bureaucracy, and specific public works issues produced sharp, inconsistent cleavage; the parties shifted their positions depending upon which was in the majority or which was in the minority. Other issues resulted in moderate or no apparent cleavage (pp. 70–71).

MacRae (1958) gave added support to the proposition that legislative parties are distinct at the roll-call stage. In order to study the Eighty-first Congress by Guttman scale analysis, MacRae was forced to use different scales of roll calls for each party (p. 222)—a "Fair Deal" scale for Democrats and a "Welfare-State" scale for Republicans.

Since Guttman scaling orders congressmen as well as votes, conflict *within* each party did not coincide with conflict *between* the parties. Carlson and Harrell (1942) factor analyzed roll-call votes in the Seventy-sixth Congress for 17 leading representatives and 17 leading senators. The first factor for the representatives was a "party" factor (p. 56) and the first senatorial factor was a "New Deal-anti New Deal" factor (p. 58). Gleeck (1940) studied voting decisions of 96 congressmen on the repeal of the arms embargo. He characterized their decision-making process as follows:

> Seldom is it an inductive process; on the contrary, the party system usually provides all but a select few who determine the party's position . . . with an orthodox answer (p. 7).

Partial correlations were used by Havens (1964) to analyze the relationship between metropolitan constituencies and foreign affairs roll-call votes. Party affiliation explained much more variance than did any other independent variable, although the major point of his investigation was that urbanism is second only to party in explaining foreign affairs votes. Marwell (1967) factor analyzed roll-call votes in the House of Representatives for the Eighty-first, Eighty-second, and Eighty-third Congresses. Even though he excluded any vote that correlated .9 or higher with party, the first factor for each of the three sessions was clearly related to party affiliation. This first factor was named, "active role of the government in society," and tended to separate the Democrats from the Republicans in spite of the fact that the roll calls selected for analysis were biased *against* party:

> The first factor in each of the analyses is correlated highly with party. The correlations are .81, .91, and .96 in the 81st, 82nd, and 83rd Congresses respectively. Thus, as would be expected, location on the most important single dimension of voting is strongly, if not perfectly, related to the most important single structural element of American political life (p. 393).

These studies establish a relationship between party affiliation and legislative voting; they did not establish the dynamics or the nature of the relationship. This failure of roll-call voting studies encouraged Crane (1960) to criticize Turner's analysis. He noted that Turner did not attempt, "to determine whether legislators were voting to uphold perceived party positions or merely responding to other factors" (p. 238). Crane then attempted to show that no correlation existed between issues that the Wisconsin state legislators identified as party votes and those that the Index of Party Likeness identified as party votes. Unfortunately, Greenstein and Jackson (1963) showed Crane's calculations to be incorrect:

> Contrary to Crane's interpretation . . . his data suggest that the IPL [Index of Party Likeness] is a reasonably valid measure of party influence (p. 159).

Fortunately, the significance of Crane's critique of roll-call studies was not wholly dependent upon his own analysis. The question he rightly raised was the criterion problem of determining the contribution of party loyalty to legislative voting; what external criteria does one use to establish the presence and strength of party influence at the roll-call stage? Crane suggested that a low Party Likeness score (meaning the party groups are quite distinct) does not justify the causal inference that party affiliation is responsible for roll-call behavior, thus the frequency of party roll calls may not be a test of the importance of party.

Crane's point is well taken; but it may be more useful if directed at roll-call research other than Turner's. Turner inferred party loyalty when the Party Likeness Index was low. As the empirical relationship continued to hold, additional controls were imposed on other plausible, causal variables, and the theoretical meaning of the party roll-call relationship was clarified and refined.

Because party has been consistently related to roll-call voting, the criterion question would seem to be more appropriately addressed to kinds of party loyalty instead of to its existence. The different measures of party in roll-call studies may, in fact, be tapping different behaviors related to the legislative party. If party commands different types of loyalty, these may be related to variation in party cleavage across issue areas.

MacRae (1956) used issues that Turner found associated with sharp, consistent party cleavage, such as social and labor issues, to produce a Guttman scale in studying ideological loyalty among Massachusetts legislators (p. 548). The issues producing sharp, inconsistent party cleavage in Turner's study, such as patronage issues, produced an organizational loyalty scale (pp. 544–548). The Democratic leadership was higher on organizational loyalty than were Republican leaders, and the Republican leadership was higher on ideological loyalty than were Democratic leaders (pp. 553–554). Party loyalty, then, was not found to be unidimensional; loyalty to the party organization and/or its ideology produce variations between the parties. In this case the legislative leaders exhibit higher loyalty than the rank and file (p. 556).

Mayhew (1966) studied roll calls in the House of Representatives from 1947–1962. His results are highly convergent with those of Mac-Rae concerning Massachusetts. On four issues—farm, city, labor, and western—it was demonstrated that the Republican party followed a strategy of supporting the party ideology which often placed congressmen from these districts under cross-pressures. Because of their emphasis upon ideology, "The likelihood is that, in these years, the Republican party in the House could be pure only at the cost of being small" (p. 163). Throughout these years, the Democrats gave support to their congressmen from each of these "interested" districts. Whereas the Democrats attempted to make party and constituency interests converge, the Republicans did not. Mayhew notes that the Democrats seemed to exemplify Rustow's (1955) inclusive pattern of legislative compromise—including the divergent elements of the party—whereas the Republicans seemed to be following the exclusive pattern—supporting a pro-business and pro-economy attitude wherever possible (Mayhew, Chapter 6).

In general, the majority party is more cohesive than the minority (Truman, 1959, p. 281; Grassmuck, 1951, p. 172; Sorauf, 1962, p. 137). Anderson (1964), however, has qualified this general proposition by proposing that cohesiveness of the majority party varies with different issues (p. 576). These different levels of cohesion may be due to the better chance majority party proposals have of being reported out of committee as compared to the chances minority proposals have (Robinson, 1962, p. 101). Thus, on final roll calls, the majority, more often than the minority, has a definite position to support. MacRae (1952, p. 1052), on the other hand, has produced evidence suggesting that not only may there be no difference between the majority and minority but that the minority may actually be more cohesive than the majority. However, this finding is not generally supported by other research.

Although party affiliation is a major consideration in legislative voting, the strength of its influence may be diluted by other factors. MacRae (1958) conceptualized legislative voting decisions as responses to relevant audiences; Truman (1959) discussed legislators who make vote decisions on the basis of cues provided by salient aspects of the legislator's environment. The general agreement is that when the party position is supported by other cues or audiences, legislators rarely vote against these pressures (Grassmuck, 1951, pp. 123–124; Turner, 1951, p. 167). When the cues or audiences place the legislator under cross-pressure, however, the effect of party affiliation is depreciated:

> Representatives subject to conflicting pressures must be able to balance these pressures, decide which ones are more important, or attempt to please all by casting conflicting votes on a succession of roll calls. In some cases, on the other hand, a congressman with conflicting pressures may be more free than others to exercise independent judgment (Turner, 1951, p. 165).

Summary

Proposition 1: Party affiliation is highly related to roll-call voting.

Proposition 2: Party loyalty is composed of loyalty to the organization and loyalty to the ideology.

Proposition 3: Democrats tend to be more loyal to the party organization than Republicans.

Proposition 4: Republicans tend to be more loyal to the party ideology than Democrats.

Proposition 5: In Congress, party loyalty tends to be stronger among members of the majority than among members of the minority.

Proposition 6: Party affiliation commands different degrees of loyalty across different issues.

Proposition 7: Party loyalty tends to be increased when party is supported by salient factors, such as region and constituency, and is decreased when opposed by salient audiences.

Proposition 8: Party leaders tend to be more loyal to the party organization and ideology than rank and file members.

THE EFFECTS OF CONSTITUENCY ON ROLL-CALL VOTING

The relationship between demographic and political characteristics of constituencies to the roll-call behavior of legislators has received considerable attention from political scientists. Such relationships may suggest important processes at work in the political system, such as the transference of felt needs from the local level to demands at the national level. Gross relationships between the political or demographic composition of a Congressional district and legislative roll calls, however, only indicate broad outlines of such processes. Inferences and propositions about legislative behavior based upon research employing gross data are limited, and these limitations must be kept in mind.

Although the underlying theory is not specified in the same terms in all places, two political scientists have described the constituency roll-call relationship:

> Because the legislator's decision is made publicly, he tries to anticipate how his decision will be viewed by relevant groups. If he acts on this knowledge, and if other legislators look to the same groups as well, then they will be deciding in terms of a common frame of reference (MacRae, 1958, p. 209).

> We then find that many people within the congressional districts share roughly similar kinds of environments. This sharing of environments, coupled with the notion that many issues affect people sharing similar environments in similar ways, leads us to the conclusion that people in similar kinds of environments are likely to share similar attitudes on many matters of public policy (Froman, 1963, p. 11).

MacRae emphasized relevant constituency groups and Froman stressed the homogeneity of the constituency environment. In either case the view is shared that congressmen pay heed to their electorate in arriving at legislative decisions. It has been a consistent conclusion of legislative research that constituency factors are related to roll-call variance (Turner, 1951; MacRae, 1952; MacRae, 1958; Froman, 1963; Froman, 1963a; Rieselbach, 1964 and 1966), and Miller and Stokes (1963) differentiate the effects of constituency across issue areas.

In explaining variation related to constituency differences, one would ideally wish to hold the effect of party constant since party is a major determinant of roll-call voting. Two studies of one-party state legislatures used such an ideal laboratory. Parsons (1962) used data on the Florida legislature from 1947–1962 to demonstrate that stable, cohesive factions were based on constituency differences; the urban, developing districts from the southern part of the state were pitted against the rural, unchanging districts from the north. Patterson (1962) studied the Oklahoma legislature to determine surrogates for party in political conflict in a one-party state. Among other findings, the political competition of the constituency was related to support for the governor's program and the socioeconomic level of the district was related to support for public education. Three factors assume increased salience for legislative conflict when inter-party competition is non-existent or held constant: (1) the level of party competition in the district, (2) socioeconomic characteristics of the constituency, and (3) the nature of the legislative issue.

The research literature reports contradictory findings relating the level of party competition to roll-call votes. Some research at the state level suggests that legislators tend to be more sensitive to constituency interests when they are elected from competitive districts (Patterson, 1961, pp. 466–467; Dye, 1961, pp. 477–478; MacRae, 1952, p. 1049). The form of this relationship varies with the specific study. Patterson and Dye maintain that competitiveness produces fewer party votes, whereas MacRae relates competitiveness of district to less extreme ideological positions. In general, these findings show that competitive districts tend to inhibit legislators from taking extreme positions in their roll-call votes.

Other research finds the reverse to be the case; the qualitative differences between the parties seem to be the greatest where inter-party competition is the smallest (Huntington, 1950, p. 669). Keefe (1956) also produced evidence to support Huntington's research; districts in which competition is closest tend to be those in which considerable difference exists between the liberalism-conservatism scores of each party. Whereas the competitive districts tended to be predominantly urban areas, the safe districts are mainly rural and the parties closer together ideologically. Miller (1962 as cited in Froman, 1963) found that congressmen from safe districts are more likely to represent district opinion than congressmen from competitive districts. In his study of the Pennsylvania legislature, Sorauf (1962, p. 139) did not discover any relationship between competitiveness based on the vote totals for each legislator and deviation from party on roll calls, but he did find a direct relationship between competitiveness based on the vote for governor and deviation from party (p. 141). In analyzing congressional voting behavior, Froman's (1963) data did not support the general hypothesis that representatives from competitive districts vote less often with their party than do those from safe districts. His data did indicate, however, that congressmen from competitive districts take less extreme ideological stands than do those from safe districts.

Before attempting to resolve the differences already outlined, it should be noted that a third variable, aside from inter-party competitiveness and roll-call behavior, was included in many of these studies. It was noted by MacRae (1952), Sorauf (1962), and Froman (1963) that the demographic composition of a district is related to legislative party loyalty, to party dominance, and to specific legislative policy-decisions. MacRae (1952) used the percent of owner-occupied dwellings to distinguish between typically Republican and typically Democratic districts. Intermediate levels of ownership tended to be competitive districts (p. 1049). It was then found that districts atypical of one's own party and more like those of the opposing party were marked by high levels of party deviancy (p. 1051).

Sorauf (1962, p. 141) also found that legislators most likely to leave party lines came from districts atypical of their party's strength. Froman (1963) used four variables to divide districts into liberal and conservative categories: percent non-white, percent owner-occupied dwellings, population per square mile, and percent urban. Democrats tended to be elected in liberal districts defined as those high in percent non-white, population per square mile, percent urban, and low in percent owner-occupied dwellings. Republicans tended to be elected from conservative constituencies identified as those low in percent non-white, population per square mile, percent urban, and high in percent owner-occupied dwellings. In areas where the legislator's party was not reinforced by type of district, he tended to follow the party vote less often, i.e., Republicans elected from urban districts adopted a more liberal voting stance than Republican colleagues from less urbanized areas.

These studies do not exhaust the research literature, but they do indicate numerous problems in its interpretation. Three sets of variables—competitiveness, party typicality of constituency, and party roll-call voting—have been studied in a variety of settings. In most cases different legislatures have been used. This in itself should increase confidence in the findings, given comparability in research design, measures, and conclusions. Unfortunately, the design, measures, and results of these studies do not converge. For this reason, the use of different legislatures only contributes another source of variance, which adds to error rather than eliminates it. It is not clear whether these studies measured the same construct, or whether the relationship of roll-call votes (the dependent variable) to competitiveness and to the demography of the district was spurious. The roll-call behavior that was measured may have been caused by other aspects of the environment or legislature that were not investigated.

In spite of these differences and the need for further research, it does seem that both competitiveness and demography of the district are related to party voting, although it is not possible to identify clearly the relationships among these three factors. One is led to the hazardous conclusion that as competitiveness increases legislators are less likely to take extreme ideological positions. The relationship between competitiveness and party voting at the national level seems to be negligible if not non-existent. At the risk of being repetitious, however, it should be noted that these two propositions have probably been confused in terms of the measures employed in some of the previous research. Finally, as districts become increasingly atypical of their party, less party loyalty tends to be exhibited. The interaction or independence of competitiveness and demography has yet to be established.

That a given political party is supported by certain groups in the electorate does not mean that any strict correspondence exists on all issues between the position of a legislative party and its supportive groups. A more interesting question than the gross relationship of demographic variables to roll calls is to what degree legislators represent the views of their constituents. Crane (1960a) compared the votes of legislators on a daylight savings time referendum with the vote of each constituency on the same referendum. Eighty-five percent of the legislators agreed with their constituents; most of the disagreement was attributed to the even division within the remaining districts so that no clear cues were provided. In some cases, the legislators were not aware of the dominant opinion in their districts (p. 248).

Miller and Stokes (1963) analyzed data from interviews with constituents, interviews with representatives, and roll-call votes on three separate issues. No relationship existed between constituency attitudes and roll-call behavior on foreign policy votes, a moderate degree of association existed on welfare issues although this was attributed to political party as an intervening variable, and finally a clear relationship was found between constituency attitudes and roll-call behavior on civil rights. Cnudde and McCrone (1966) subjected the same civil rights data to Simon-Blalock causal analysis[1] demonstrating that the causal mechanism was the representative's perception of the constituency's attitude as opposed to an alternative theory of elite recruitment. The candidate did not necessarily share the attitude with the constituency but he based his vote on his perception of the district's attitude. These studies indicate that the degree of constituency influence is issue specific, exhibiting considerable strength on some roll calls while being completely absent on others.

Summary

Proposition 9: Political and demographic characteristics of legislative districts are related to roll-call behavior.

Proposition 10: Inter-party competitiveness in state legislatures tends to be related to fewer party votes and inhibits legislators from taking extreme ideological positions.

Proposition 11: Inter-party competitiveness in the House of Representatives does not seem to be related to party voting but does decrease the tendency for representatives to take extreme ideological positions.

Proposition 12: Legislative districts atypical of party strength tend to produce less party loyalty at the roll-call stage.

Proposition 13: The relationship between constituency and roll-call voting tends to be issue specific; the areas of greatest influence are on affairs within the district and the weakest influence is on affairs outside the district.

Proposition 14: Party dominance tends to be related to the demographic variables of owner-occupied housing, population per square mile, percent non-white, and percent urban.

---

[1] Simon-Blalock causal analysis is a method by which causal inferences relating two or more variables can be made. This is to be distinguished from correlational analysis which is not designed to systematically test causal statements. See Hubert Blalock, Jr., *Causal Inferences in Nonexperimental Research* (Chapel Hill: The University of North Carolina Press, 1964).

Sectionalism and Congressional Voting

Roach (1925) was one of the first to study the importance of sectionalism in Congressional roll-call voting. She concluded that from 1870–1890, "Sectionalism is a fundamental and persistent factor in American politics" (p. 500). Sectionalism did not exert a consistent influence upon roll-call voting but it became more important during economic crisis, whereas party voting increased in times of prosperity (p. 503). Sectional divisions followed a similar pattern. In each party, the North Atlantic states took a conservative position and the West and South a radical position on economic policy (p. 518).

Grassmuck (1951) studied sectionalism and foreign policy roll calls from 1921–1941. In one respect, he reached the same general conclusion as Roach, "When party unity does break down, the cause is usually sectionalism" (p. 14). Grassmuck also supported Roach's finding concerning sectional cleavage within each party. On foreign policy the Democrats were split between the North and the South with the border states as the battleground. The lake states of Ohio, Michigan, Indiana, and Illinois formed a transition area between the East and the West within the Republican party (p. 157). Generally the Northeast favored increased international participation, whereas the South preferred policies designed to bring success to the Democratic party (p. 102). The Midwest was opposed to military and naval armaments, alliances, and entanglements (p. 170). In addition to outlining the existence and nature of sectional cleavage, Grassmuck noted that sectional attitudes change in intensity as issues change and as time passes (p. 14).

Key (1949) investigated roll-call votes of southern senators and representatives in his classic study, *Southern Politics*. He found that party and regional associations produced more cohesion among representatives than among senators (p. 370). Despite Turner's finding that party explains more roll-call votes than any other variable, Key found that region for southern Democrats produced higher cohesion than was found in either party. Race was the major concern (pp. 350ff., 370ff.) in those issues where region explained the cohesion of the southerners against non-southern Democrats and Republicans.

Westerfield (1955) found definite effects of region on foreign policy voting:

It was evident at once and confirmed by various checks that within each party there were significant regional variations. This was true in the Democratic party between North and South, with the Mountains going along with the South. It was even more true in the Republican party, between the two Coasts and the Interior (p. 32).

Rieselbach (1964) studied the demography of Congressional voting on foreign aid from 1939–1958. During this period party declined in importance as region and constituency became more closely associated with foreign aid votes:

. . . the important point here is that with the passage of time the importance of single variables as correlates of voting behavior may ebb and flow (p. 579).

Marwell (1967) has reported effects of party and region in the House of Representatives from 1949 to 1954. His factor analysis of roll-call votes demonstrated that the dimensions of conflict remained relatively constant during these years. With but one exception, the first three factors or dimensions of roll-call voting were named "Active Role of Government in Society," "Protection of Private or Local Interests," and "Foreign Aid." The exception occurred during the Eighty-second Congress which convened during the Korean War. At this time the third factor was more appropriately labeled "Foreign Involvement." "The second and third factors are primarily defined by cleavages within one party or the other" (p. 394). The second factor, which included votes on Negro civil rights was related to the North-South split among Democrats. On the "Foreign Aid/Involvement" factor there was a split between coastal and midwest Republicans, but all midwestern congressmen did not oppose foreign aid. Midwest Democrats did not vote with their own group. It is evident that sectionalism does not explain roll-call behavior independently of party, for the composition of each party has a distinctive relation to region.

In his study of *The Congressional Party*, Truman (1959) discovered that regional variation within each party had different effects on voting cohesion:

There was among the Republicans no single and sharp line of cleavage such as that which divided the northern from the southern wing of the House Democrats, but rather a series of noncongruent tendencies within the party, reflected shifting and fluid bases of agreement and, presumably, of association (p. 173).

Truman supports the evident and often reported finding concerning the northern and southern Democrats, but he does not support the statements concerning regional variation within the Republican party. To completely discount the research relating coastal and midwest Republicans to foreign aid roll calls, however, does not seem warranted.

It is not clear what the intervening process is that converts regional affiliation into a roll-call vote. It is clear, however, that regional interests constitute an audience that provide cues to congressmen at the roll-call stage.

Summary

Proposition 15:   The sectional base of a congressman tends to be related to his roll-call voting.

Proposition 16:   As party unity decreases on roll calls within the House of Representatives cohesion within regional groups tends to increase.

Proposition 17:   Intra-party conflict within the Democratic party in the House of Representatives tends to be associated with cleavage between northern and southern representatives.

Proposition 18:   Intra-party conflict within the Republican party tends to be less consistent and less associated with region than within the Democratic party.

Proposition 19:   Intra-party conflict within the Republican party exists between coastal and midwestern congressmen.

Proposition 20:   As the relationship between party and votes on foreign aid has declined, the relationship between region and foreign aid voting has increased.

THE REPRESENTATIVE AND ROLL-CALL VOTING

Bailey (1950) conducted an extensive analysis of the Full Employment Bill of 1946, and described the legislative process thus:

Legislative policy-making appears to be the result of a confluence of factors streaming from an almost endless number of tributaries (p. 236).

The foregoing analyses of Congressional voting focused on influences pushing and pulling the representative this way and that. The congressman, himself, however, brings to Congress political predispositions. He is by no means an impersonal object batted about by impersonal forces.

Froman (1963a) looked at the importance of the individual in Congressional voting. He reviewed reciprocal trade legislation in the House from 1948–1958. Variance attributable to party was eliminated by selecting only constituencies represented by one party. These single party districts were divided into single occupancy, in which one member represented the district for the entire period, and multiple occupancy districts. Voting for reciprocal trade among the multiple occupancy districts was clearly not as stable as in single occupancy districts. Individuality produced more variance among Democrats than among Republicans, more variance among southern Democrats than among northern Democrats, more variance in close, competitive districts than in safe ones, and more variance in higher socioeconomic status districts than in low ones (p. 331).

Garceau and Silverman (1954) and Silverman (1954) demonstrated that legislators have a variety of conceptions of legislative conflict. They identified four basic perceptions of legislative conflict in the 1951 session of the Vermont legislature: (1) there was no uniting theme in the session, (2) factional conflict existed, (3) conflict centering on the governor's program was perceived, and (4) conflict existed around broad policy alternatives (pp. 682–683). Legislators with longer service, more formal education, and less geographic isolation were related positively to viewing the legislative process in more complex terms (p. 687).

Silverman (1954) asked Massachusetts legislators about the most visible features of the legislative process. Party turned out to be the most visible factor on which legislators held three basic conceptions: (1) the parties were polarized in terms of social and economic issues, (2) they were defined in terms of party leaders, and (3) they were seen in both ideological and organizational terms (pp. 184–185). An explicit positive relationship existed between the legislators' view of party and the visibility of interest group activity (p. 186). Representatives who saw party as a combination of organization and ideology also saw interest group activity most clearly; those who saw party in only an ideological context were least able to identify interest group activity. In this study those who saw party in social-class terms corresponded to those in the Vermont study who had the narrowest perception of legislative processes (pp. 187–188).

Brimhall and Otis (1948) have shown that legislators tend to be consistent in their voting patterns. Senators and representatives were assigned a liberal-conservative scale score based on their roll-call votes. During the Congressional sessions from 1944–1947, 46 percent of the legislators did not change their scale position, 83 percent did not change their position over one unit on the seven unit scale, and 95 percent did not change over two units (p. 1). The *group* as a whole could have shifted its position, but *within* the group voting consistency was very high. Marwell (1967) also found that in cases where a representative served in more than one of the Eighty-first, Eighty-second, or Eighty-third Congresses, his roll-call votes were highly consistent (p. 390).

Consistency in legislative voting is to be expected, however, because roll-call votes have been related to party affiliation, region, constituency type, and the individual's predisposition or ideology. For any given representative, these factors are likely to be constant during his tenure as a legislator.

Summary

Proposition 21: The political predispositions or ideologies of congressmen are related to roll-call voting even when the effects of party, region, and constituency are controlled.

Proposition 22: Congressmen differentially perceive a wide range of conflict in a legislature; longer legislative service, more formal education and less geographic isolation are related to viewing legislative conflict in complex terms.

Proposition 23: Legislators with a narrow perception of legislative conflict tend to be less aware of interest group activity and high on ideological loyalty to the party.

Proposition 24: Legislators tend to be very consistent in their roll-call votes from one Congressional session to the next.

LEGISLATIVE PROCESSES AND CONGRESSIONAL VOTING

Recently, increased attention has been given to the characteristics of legislatures as social systems. Research on legislative processes and norms, however, does not lend itself to the same kind of analysis as does the use of discrete variables. These studies have concentrated on analyzing legislatures as systems of interaction rather than using roll-call votes as dependent variables.

COMMUNICATION IN A LEGISLATURE

Routt (1938) conducted one of the first investigations of inter-personal interactions in a legislative body. He observed personal inter-actions in the Illinois General Assembly:

Preliminary inspection of the tabulations of these contacts indicates that contacts tended to center around individuals who by other indices were shown to play important roles in the process of legislation, although those with the longest legislative careers showed no important deviation from the norm of the group (p. 132).

Although lines and frequency of communications do not necessarily parallel patterns of influence, consultations and interactions may well outline the flow of policy-making in a legislature. Routt found minor-ity members conferring with majority leaders more frequently than majority members conferred with minority leaders. Although only six Democrats and five Republicans constituted the group of legislators that was observed, more than 65 percent of the total contacts occurred within the majority party, 25 percent between the majority and the minority, and less than 10 percent of the total occurred within the ranks of the minority party (p. 135). Four of the legislators observed were neophytes who had less than four years seniority, and seven were experienced members. Contact among the experienced members accounted for 48 percent of the total, contact among experienced and neophyte members accounted for 45 percent, and only 7 percent of the contacts was within the neophyte group (p. 136). This study strongly suggests that influence is centered among the majority leaders, the majority members, and the experienced members.

Wahlke and his associates (1962) found that friendship groups in a legislature tend to be limited in size (pp. 224ff.). They discovered that friendship choices did not seem to perform any integrating func-tion; rather veteran members chose veterans, and freshmen chose fresh-men. Choices also tended to follow and to not cross party lines, enhancing rather than breaking down party conflict. This type of friendship pattern offers a partial explanation for the interactions recorded by Routt. When it came to voting, members gave a high degree of support to legislation proposed by their friends. On the other hand, when party and length of service were held constant, friendship choices accounted for an additional 9 percent of the voting variance. Thus it was concluded that friendships do have an effect on legislative policy-making.

Patterson (1959) supported one of Routt's findings when he interviewed members of the Wisconsin Assembly. Leaders tended to be chosen much more as friends when compared to the average member. Apparently members with lesser authority identified psychologically with the leaders (pp. 108–109).

Francis (1962) employed the reputational method for determining influential members of the Indiana Senate. He supported another of Routt's earlier conclusions:

> . . . there is a direct relationship between length of service and degree of influence. . . (p. 954).

He also found a high, positive relationship between general influencers and high interactors (p. 956).

Truman (1956) and Fiellin (1962) addressed the question of cohesion and interaction within state delegations in the House of Representatives. Truman, by using Rice-Beyle cluster bloc analysis,[2] did not directly attack the problem of interactions, but his findings are suggestive for those interested in studying informal groups within the legislative system. High intra-state cohesion was inversely related to high party cohesion. It was proffered that when the party does not give cues or the cues are not strong enough, members seek other sources in making voting decisions. Truman comments:

> The [state] delegation thus tends to constitute a communication structure whose repeated use results in a heightened consensus and similarity of voting among its members (p. 1024).

[2] Stuart Rice developed a method of identifying blocs of legislators which was later modified by Herman Beyle. The Rice-Beyle cluster bloc analysis permits investigators to identify empirically blocs of legislators based on the degree of internal agreement of the bloc members on roll-call votes. For a more complete discussion see, Lee Anderson, Meredith Watts, Jr., and Allen Wilcox, *Legislative Roll-Call Analysis* (Evanston: Northwestern University Press, 1966), Chapter 4.

Fiellin studied the New York State Democratic delegation in the House of Representatives and found that communication among New York Democrats served three purposes: (1) it provided "trustworthy" information, (2) it provided cues for making voting decisions, and (3) it provided adaptive norms, perceptions, and rationalizations (p. 178). Fiellin concluded:

> . . . it is hypothesized that House politics is not unintelligibly complex consisting only of individual behavior of each of 435 isolated members. Rather, it is much more simply structured through a network of informal groups and relationships (p. 90).

Fiellin's findings are supported by other studies in this area, and they note, as one could expect, that informal groups conform to a very high degree to the formal groups in a legislature.

Research on intra-legislative communications suggests relationships to legislative research discussed earlier. If more than half of the contacts within a legislature occur among members of the majority party, it is not surprising that the majority votes with greater cohesion than the minority, other variables notwithstanding. If there is some rough parallel between frequency of contacts and information transmitted, it is not surprising that the number of contacts might be related to a more complex perception of legislative conflict, despite length of service. Communication nets in a legislature certainly do not offer a very thorough or complete explanation of roll-call behavior; they do appear, however, to be related to roll-call choices.

It would seem, then, that:

a) Differential communication rates within the parties are related to the higher voting cohesion of the majority party.

b) Differential communication rates related to length of service would seem to be related to the differential perception of the complexity of political conflict in a legislature.

These two notions are not supported by extant research, but instead seem plausible in light of legislative studies.

Summary

Proposition 25:   Frequency of communication is higher among majority than among minority members in a legislature.

Proposition 26: Frequency of communication is higher among experienced members than among neophytes.

Proposition 27: There tends to be a high, positive relationship between high influencers and high interactors.

Proposition 28: State delegations tend to have a higher than average amount of interaction and voting cohesion in the House of Representatives.

Proposition 29: Friendship groups do not tend to perform an integrating function in a legislature.

LEGISLATIVE NORMS

Matthews (1960) conducted an extensive study of legislative norms. The standards to which senators are expected to conform are: (1) apprenticeship, (2) legislative work, (3) specialization, (4) courtesy, (5) reciprocity, and (6) institutional patriotism (pp. 92–102). Again we find overlap with other legislative research. Whereas Routt (1938) found a high frequency of communication among experienced members, and lower frequencies of communication among experienced members and neophytes, and among neophyte members themselves. Matthews notes:

The first rule of Senate behavior, and the one most widely recognized off the Hill, is that new members are expected to serve a proper apprenticeship. . . . Moreover, the new senator is expected to keep his mouth shut, not to take the lead in floor fights, to listen and to learn (pp. 92, 93).

As previously discussed, Francis (1962) found legislative influence spreading from one area of competence to other areas. Matthews states:

According to the folkways of the Senate, a senator should not try to know something about every bill that comes before the chamber nor try to be active on a wide variety of measures (p. 95).

One might expect that the norm of specialization would be related to an influence pattern in which influence spreads from one area of competence to that of general influence. Matthews also found a direct, positive relationship between conformity to Senate norms and legislative "effectiveness" (pp. 114–115).

In the classic state legislative study by Wahlke, Eulau, Buchanan, and Ferguson (1962), legislators were in agreement on the "rules of the game." These rules performed the functions of (1) promoting group cohesion and solidarity, (2) increasing the predictability of legislative behavior, (3) channeling and restraining conflict, and (4) expediting legislative business (p. 155). The rules were not random customs, but informal norms that systematically developed to complement the more formal procedures and structure of the legislative body.

The centrality of the leaders in informal interactions has already been established. Wahlke and his associates demonstrated that members *expect* the leaders to focus issues and resolve conflict by disseminating information and by administering the system so that it will be stable and predictable. Specialization is a widely accepted practice, and a high degree of correspondence exists between informal and formal specialization. Length of service and amount of formal education are strongly and positively related to expertise; this agrees with Francis' findings.

Fenno (1962) studied legislative norms operative in congressional committees. The House Appropriations Committee has a number of processes designed to socialize new members and maintain continued integration. The committee's norms, which were in part adapted from the legislature as a whole, were, (1) specialization, (2) reciprocity (which meant deference to each subcommittee's report), (3) subcommittee unity, and (4) minimal partisanship (pp. 316–317). New members gain influence by supporting the leaders, in return they acquire intra-committee influence. Deviant members are brought around by the socializing process of committee hearings, which tends to induce the dominant goal of cutting budget estimates and guarding the treasury (p. 320). A second process for minimizing deviant behavior are the intra-committee sanctions that may be applied. These, in general, are the denial, by other members of the committee, of deference, reciprocity, and, ultimately, influence (p. 321).

On the basis of Truman's Rice-Beyle cluster bloc analysis (1959), he described Congressional parties as mediate groups:

> ... meaning that the relations constituting the groups are distinctively affected but not wholly determined by their members' affiliations with and dependence upon other groups (p. 293).

Thus, very real limits exist on a member's loyalty to his legislative party. Even maintenance of his legislator's status is dependent upon continued support from his constituency which may conflict with party demands. The mediate nature of Congressional parties produced interesting results in terms of voting cohesion:

1) leaders tended to be near the middle of their parties (p. 205), and

2) committees did not provide cues producing high cohesion among their members (p. 272).

Fenno (1962) and Farnsworth (1961), however, support the alternative contention that committees provide effective cues to committee members on bills reported out of their committees. Fenno has noted that the House Appropriations Committee makes a special effort to achieve unanimity on legislation sent to the House floor. Farnsworth demonstrated that new members to the Senate Foreign Relations Committee tended, "to assume the attitudes already shared by the older committee members" (p. 175). Truman argued that for the Eighty-first Congress cohesion within committees on measures they reported to the floor, "in most cases fluctuated directly with the cohesion of the parties . . ." (p. 273). Apparently committees, at certain times, provide significant cues to their members in their area of specialization; at other times, cues from the party dominate those from the committee.

We may, at this point, infer generalizations concerning when committee cues are operative and when they are not. Truman studied all the legislative committees in Congress and concluded that they had limited explanatory power at the roll-call stage. Both Fenno and Farnsworth examined highly prominent, powerful committees and came to the opposite conclusion. It may be hypothesized that these different findings are related to the differential integration of legislative committees. Fenno (1962) suggests that integration may be explained by: (1) the existence of a well-articulated and deeply rooted consensus on committee goals and tasks, (2) the nature of the committee's subject matter, (3) the legislative orientation of its members, (4) the attractiveness of the committee for its members, and (5) stability of the committee's membership. Farnsworth's study (1961) is suggestive of an important socialization process leading new members of the Senate Foreign Relations Committee to share the attitudes of the older members. It is not likely that these important committee characteristics and processes are, nor can they be, shared by all Congressional committees. Because high committee cohesion accompanies highly integrated committees in these instances, it is reasonable to assume that voting cohesion is a product of integration. This will be our working assumption until further contradictory research is at hand.

Finally, in concluding this section, a comparison of intra-legislative communications and norms finds them related as follows:

a) Infrequent contacts among new legislators seem to be related to the norm of apprenticeship.

b) A pattern of influence that spreads from one area of competence to another seems related to the norm of specialization.

c) The central position of legislative leaders in legislative communications would seem to be related to the general expectations among members that they are to focus and resolve political conflict.

Summary

Proposition 30: Legislative norms focus on (1) apprenticeship, (2) legislative work, (3) specialization, (4) courtesy, (5) reciprocity, and (6) institutional patriotism.

Proposition 31: Legislative norms perform the functions of (1) promoting group cohesion and solidarity, (2) increasing the predictability of legislative behavior, (3) channeling and restraining conflict, and (4) expediting legislative business.

Proposition 32: Legislators tend toward high agreement on legislative norms.

Proposition 33: There is a direct, positive relationship between conformity to legislative norms and legislative effectiveness.

Proposition 34: Legislators expect their leaders to focus issues and resolve conflict by the dissemination of information.

Proposition 35: Legislators expect their leaders to administer the system so that it will be stable and predictable.

Proposition 36: Norms operative in a legislative committee are partially adopted from the norms of the legislature as a whole.

Proposition 37:   The integration of legislative committees is related to (1) the existence of a well-articulated and established set of goals, (2) the nature of the committee's subject matter, (3) the legislative orientation of its members, (4) the attractiveness of the committee for its members, and (5) stability of its membership.

Proposition 38:   Well-integrated committees give voting cues to members that tend to be followed at the roll-call stage.

Proposition 39:   All legislative committees do not provide cues that produce high cohesion among their members on roll-call votes.

Proposition 40:   Voting cohesion among committee members tends to be inversely correlated with voting among members of the legislative party.

A STRATEGY FOR BUILDING A MODEL OF LEGISLATIVE ROLL-CALL VOTING

In his analysis of the fight for majority leader between Carl Albert and Richard Bolling, Polsby (1963) employed a very useful and suggestive classification scheme. He noted that the two aspirants followed different strategies in pushing their cases; Albert followed an "inside" strategy and Bolling an "outside" one.

The inside strategy is likely to define situations as "family matters," and feature face-to-face interaction among members. The outside strategy is likely to evoke a more ideological, issue-oriented definition of the situation (p. 268).

Eulau and Hinckley (1966) expanded the "inside-outside" distinction to develop two models to provide the theoretical orientation of their review of the legislative behavior research:

The first of these, which might be termed the "inside model," concerns legislative behavior and action as revealed in the growth of formal and informal substructures, groups, authority relations, influence patterns, and so on, within the legislature. The "outside model" conceives the legislature's and the legislator's activities as products of forces or influences beyond the institutional boundaries of the legislature—the electoral constitutencies, district parties, pressure groups, executive agencies, and those socioeconomic and predispositional attributes that legislators import from the "outside" (p. 87).

These two models seem to provide useful and valid guidelines for the construction of a computer simulation of legislative voting. The previous discussion of legislative research indicates that factors outside the legislature present different considerations than do formal and informal processes within the legislature.

The model of legislative voting described in the next two chapters concerns two models of legislative behavior. One model, the individual stage, represents factors such as party affiliation, constituency, region, and predispositions. It structures relationships impinging upon legislators from the extra-legislative environment.

The second sub-model in the computer program is closely related to the "inside model." The communication stage programs interactions among congressmen and the influence of these communications. Authority and influence tend to be associated with interaction and interactions tend to follow certain patterns (Propositions 25, 26, and 27). One may think of the "outside model" or individual phase as an initial distribution of predispositions toward a given roll call (see Chapter 3). The "inside model" or communication phase then, subjects this initial distribution to changes simulating interaction and influence *within* the House (see Chapter 4). As a result of these operations, a final distribution of simulated roll-call votes is produced.

Simulating Voting Predispositions of United States Representatives

Our simulation model of roll-call voting in the House of Representatives focuses on two basic processes. The first is a cognitive process involving the development of a representative's predisposition toward a bill as he (1) assesses his own past voting behavior on that type of bill, (2) assesses the positive or negative position toward the bill of individuals and groups in the House, and (3) assesses the substance of the bill in terms of its benefits and disadvantages for his constituency and region of the country. The second is a communication process in which representatives who do not develop strong predispositions on a bill in the first phase of the model, confront the president and their colleagues and receive influence. The sequence of the model as it operates when a bill is entered is presented in the flow chart of Figure 1.

The communication phase of the model is explained, step by step, in Chapter 4. This chapter presents a description of the structure and theoretical basis of the predisposition phase. We begin by indicating how this phase fits into the modeling strategy as a whole.

The basic elements of a simulation model are components, variables (including input, output, and status variables), and relationships (Orcutt, 1960). The components of our model are the members of the House. These components are defined by *status variables*. In our simulation model, variables suggested by the research literature, such as party affiliation and region, are used to characterize each member of the House.

Roll-call votes constitute *input and output variables*; these, too, may be defined by status variables. Roll calls in our simulation model are defined by such status variables as the party introducing the vote, and regional support or opposition for the roll call. The status variables that define each congressman and each roll-call vote correspond closely but they are not identical.

On the basis of *relationships* which structure the components and variables, the individual stage of the model calculates predisposition scores based on each representative's confrontation with a given roll call. The output of the individual stage, then, consists of a predisposition score for each representative on the roll call that is being processed.

Congressmen with weak predispositions (i.e., those with a low predisposition score) confront all 434 of their colleagues, and in some cases the president, in the communication stage. Such congressmen are undecided and, consequently, are susceptible to influence as interpersonal interactions in the House are simulated. As a result of these simulated interactions, representatives develop new predispositions upon which their vote is based. When the individual votes of our simulated representatives are aggregated, we will have simulated the roll-call process of the House.

MEMBERS OF THE HOUSE AND STATUS VARIABLES

The status variables used to define each representative and the propositions upon which their selection was based are:[1]

(1) Party. Proposition 1: Party affiliation is highly related to roll-call voting (Turner, 1951, p. 23; Turner, 1951a, p. 145; Froman, 1963, p. 88).

[1] See Chapter 2 for a discussion of these propositions.

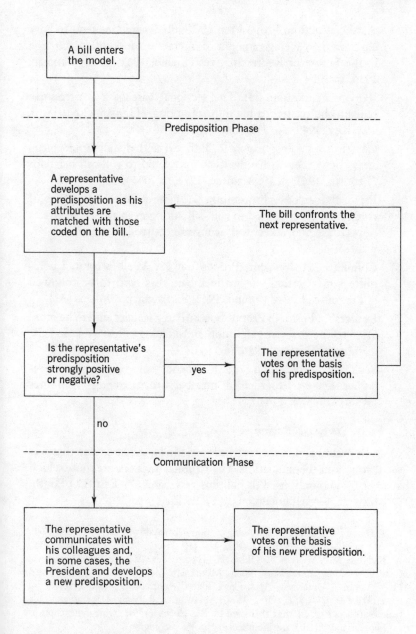

FIGURE 1. The Two Phases of the Model

(2)   State Delegation. Proposition 28: State delegations tend to have a higher than average amount of interaction and voting cohesion in the House of Representatives (Fiellin, 1962, p. 78; Truman, 1956, p. 1024).

(3)   Region. Proposition 15: The sectional base of a congressman tends to be related to his roll-call voting (Grassmuck, 1951, p. 102; Key, 1949, pp. 350ff and 370ff.).

(4)   Constituency. Proposition 9: Political and demographic characteristics of legislative districts are related to roll-call behavior (Froman, 1963, p. 59; MacRae, 1952, p. 1051).

(5)   Personal Ideology. Proposition 21: The political ideologies of congressmen are related to roll-call voting even when the effects of party, region, and constituency are controlled (Froman, 1963, p. 107).

(6)   Committee Assignment. Proposition 38: Well-integrated committees give voting cues to members that tend to be followed at the roll-call stage (Fenno, 1962; Farnsworth, 1961, p. 175).

(7)   Leadership Position. Proposition 8: Party leaders tend to be more loyal to the party organization and ideology than rank and file members (MacRae, 1956, p. 556).

(8)   Seniority. Proposition 26: Frequency of communication is higher among experienced members than among neophytes (Routt, 1938, p. 136).

Party, State, and Region

Both parties and each state were assigned a specific code that was used throughout the simulation. The regional divisions are those which have been commonly used in political research: (1) East, (2) South, (3) Midwest, (4) Mountain, and (5) Pacific.[2]

[2] The model used the following regional breakdown: *East*—Conn., Del., Me., Mass., N.H., N.J., N.Y., Pa., R.I., Vt. (10 states); *South*—Ala., Ark., Fla., Ga., Ky., La., Md., Miss., N.C., Okla., S.C., Tenn., Tex., Va., W. Va. (15 states); *Midwest*—Ill., Ind., Iowa, Kan., Mich., Minn., Mo., Neb., N.D., Ohio, S.D., and Wis. (12 states); *Mountain*—Ariz., Colo., Idaho, Mont., Nev., N.M., Utah, Wyo. (8 states); *Pacific*—Calif., Ore., Wash., Hawaii, and Alaska (5 states). This breakdown is patterned after that used by Rieselbach (1964), with the exception that Hawaii and Alaska are included in the Pacific region.

Constituency

Proposition 8 states the well-known relationship between variations among legislative districts and the roll-call votes of their legislators. Nine variables defined each congressional district in the simulation
model: (1) urban, (2) rural non-farm, (3) rural, (4) Negro, (5)
foreign stock, (6) owner-occupied dwellings, (7) white collar, (8)
plurality of the incumbent, and (9) inter-party competitiveness.[3]

The two issue areas in which roll calls were simulated were
(1) expansion of the federal role, and (2) foreign affairs. Froman
(1963, p. 114) used the expansion of the federal role to test the
hypothesis concerning ideological positions. Research has indicated
that foreign affairs tends to be an ideological issue (Rieselbach,
1966).

Percentage figures for these district attributes were not included
in the simulation model. Two reasons underlay the decision to group
the constituencies into ordinal categories. First, the research literature
discussed in Chapter 2 does not report findings with the strength or
consistency that warrants the use of interval input data. We have seen
that the conclusions of the separate studies on inter-party competition
are contradictory, in some aspects, and the amount of explained variance is small. Rieselbach (1966) in his investigation of votes on foreign

[3] The cut-off points for these variables are (1) *percent urban*—below and
including 45% was low, 46% through 70% was medium, and above 70% was
high; (2) *percent rural non-farm*—below 25% was low and 25% and above
was high; (3) *percent rural*—below 7% was low and 7% and above was high;
(4) *percent Negro*—below 10% was low and 10% and above was high; (5)
percent foreign stock—below 22% was low and 22% and above was high; (6)
percent owner-occupied dwellings—below 55% was low, from 55% to 70% was
medium, and 70% and above was high; (7) *percent white collar*—below 30% was
low, from 30% through 39% was low medium, from 40% through 49% was
high medium, and 50% and above was high; (8) *plurality of the incumbent*—
below 55% of the vote was low, from 55% through 60% was medium, and
above 60% was high; and (9) *inter-party competitiveness*—it was classified as a
safe district if the same party had controlled the constituency for the previous
four elections; if not, it was classified as a competitive district. These cut-off
points were derived by inspecting and dividing each distribution at what seemed
to be the mid-point of the natural break and not in terms of any statistical division such as a quartile or median. The raw data was obtained from the *Congressional District Data Book, Districts of the 88th Congress*, 1963.

aid in the House of Representatives demonstrates that (1) the relationship between constituency and voting behavior changes as time passes, and (2) the nominal categories of isolationist and internationalist explain considerable variation among the attributes of congressmen. Rieselbach's work exemplifies the practice of dividing congressmen, on the basis of their votes or other characteristics, into nominal and ordinal classes for the purpose of analysis. Because, as mentioned previously, simulation models are heavily dependent upon prior research, it is not possible to justify the use of finer distinctions than was found in the research. Reliance upon interval data to classify congressional districts would also have been misleading by suggesting a non-existent rigor in the model.

A second but related reason for grouping districts into ordinal classes is that it facilitated the use of the computer model. Had the constituencies been tagged with precise percentages on each of the nine attributes selected, extremely arbitrary decisions would have been called for in relating the strength of a specific variable to a particular roll call. For example, if one district is 60 percent urban and another 65 percent urban and the vote on an education bill is to be simulated, a question similar to this arises: Will both districts be coded in favor of the bill? Or will the 65 percent urban district be more in favor of the measure than the 60 percent urban district? The consequence of using interval data to describe constituencies, given the present level of our research, would have eventually led to decisions based on ordinal considerations. A high urban district tends to be operationally defined in the literature in the same way, whether the study focuses on foreign aid or domestic roll calls. The precision of legislative research, therefore, determines the precision of the model. This same argument also applies to the weights assigned in the predisposition phase of the simulation and to other parts of the model.

Committee Assignment and Leadership Position

It has been established that some structural-organizational features of a legislative body are related to roll-call behavior. Proposition 8 states that the party leadership tends to be cohesive and more supportive of the party compared to non-leaders. This model is constructed so that elected leaders give the party more support than non-elected leaders or non-leaders.

Proposition 11: Inter-party competitiveness in the House of Representatives does not seem to be related to party voting but does decrease the tendency for representatives to take extreme ideological positions.

This proposition led to the differential weighting of safe and competitive constituencies. The hypothesis was operationalized by doubling the influence of competitive constituencies in relation to safe districts. This had the effect of decreasing the importance of the individual predisposition of congressmen in determining their roll-call votes.

Proposition 38 notes that Congressional committees may be differentiated by the amount of cohesion exhibited on the bills reported out for final roll calls. This proposition demanded flexibility of the model depending upon the committee(s) involved. The committee assignments of each representative were included in his list of attributes. If the simulator considered these committees to be highly integrated, bills input into the simulation related to these committees could be coded to produce increased cohesion among the committee members. Committees with low levels of integration could also be coded to produce cohesion no higher than average. Decisions concerning committee integration were based on the research literature, such as the findings of Fenno (1962) and Farnsworth (1961).

Personal Ideology

It is well known that American political parties do not command the strict obedience of their members (American Political Science Association Committee on Political Parties, 1951). Whether an individual's political views are described as his ideology (Farris, 1958), in terms of habit strength (Eysenck, 1954), or as a network of attitudes (Newcomb, Turner, and Converse, 1965), it is clear that the behavior of a legislator may not result from impersonal forces acting upon him (Froman, 1963a; Brimhall and Otis, 1948). A legislator may express his personal beliefs in his roll-call behavior; it has been shown, however, that a representative cannot ignore his party or constituency with complete immunity (Turner, 1951, p. 175).

The quantification of a representative's ideological position assumes the existence of and the ability to identify dimensions of legislative ideology. Farris (1958), Belknap (1958), MacRae (1958), and

Brimhall and Otis (1948) have supported both of these assumptions by assigning legislators an ideological position on the basis of their roll-call votes. These studies made two points. First, they indicated that only a few dimensions are required to describe a legislator's personal ideology or "memory"; MacRae (1958) used only five scales each for Republicans and Democrats in his study of the Eighty-eighth Congress. Second, it was shown that the roll-call votes of congressmen tend to be very consistent from one session of Congress to the next (Brimhall and Otis, 1948).

Proposition 24:   Legislators tend to be very consistent in their roll-call votes from one legislative session to the next.

For these reasons, roll calls from the previous session of Congress—the Eighty-seventh—were used to represent personal ideology or memory in our simulation model.

Separate tests of the unidimensionality of the bills simulated were made to determine empirically whether both the foreign and domestic bills could be considered to be related to distinct ideological dimensions in the Eighty-eighth Congress. A representative's ideological predisposition was calculated in the model on the basis of the number of times he voted in support of foreign affairs or for an increase in the federal role as a proportion of all such bills on which his vote was recorded. Ideological scores, then, existed for incumbents at the beginning of each simulation run. There were 71 new representatives in the Eighty-eighth Congress. Their votes cast became operative as their memory only after they had been recorded on at least 10 roll calls in an issue area. The calculation of memory as each bill was processed by the simulation model included an updating procedure so that the voting behavior of the representative on a given bill would affect his ideological posture on the next bill in that issue area.

A second proposition incorporated in the ideological scores for each congressman was related less to previous legislative research than to research on attitude strength.

Proposition 41:   Persons (legislators) who hold extreme positions are less susceptible to counter-influences than are individuals who hold moderate positions (Converse, 1962; Hovland, Harvey, and Sherif, 1957).

Differential predisposition scores were assigned to congressmen on the basis of whether their past support of the administration was extreme or moderate.

Members of the House and Status Variables as Data

A separate IBM card—435 in all—was used to represent each member of the House of Representatives when the data was fed into the computer. Figure 2 illustrates how data was recorded for processing; seniority is the only variable shown that has not been discussed already; it is not related to the individual stage of the model.

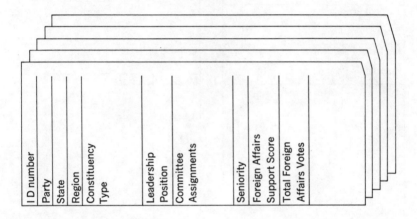

FIGURE 2. The Data Deck

Roll Calls as Inputs

Legislative bills or motions at the roll-call stage are simulation inputs. These measures are defined by variables inducing legislative predispositions toward them. The variables characterizing roll calls are: (1) party introducing the roll call, (2) states favorably affected by it, (3) regions favoring or opposing it, (4) types of constituencies supporting or opposing it, (5) the committee reporting the measure, (6) members of the committee signing a minority report, (7) whether a high support score would favor or oppose the vote, and (8) the party, region, and state of the president. Not all of these variables are used to define each roll-call vote.

Whereas only one IBM data card is used for each representative in the simulation, two data cards are used for each roll call. The arrangement of roll-call input data is shown in Figure 3.

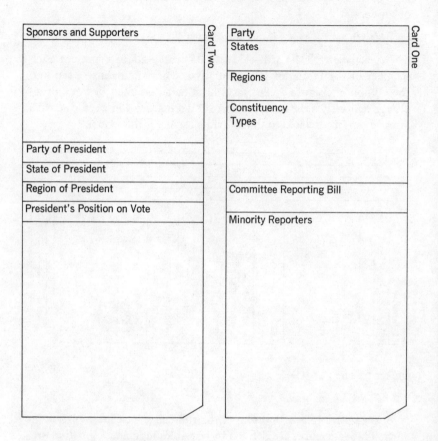

FIGURE 3. The Input Deck

An example from the Eighty-eighth Congress illustrates the way roll calls are coded. HR 7885 authorized the foreign aid appropriation for 1964. This bill was coded as a Democratic bill because it was proposed by the Democratic administration. Because it was a foreign aid bill and not concerned with any domestic issue, it was not coded as salient to any state, region, or constituency.[4] The House Foreign Af-

[4] Experiments were conducted that treated certain regions and constituencies as salient to foreign aid (see Chapter 8).

fairs Committee was coded as reporting the bill out and the state, region, and party of the president were placed in the communication system so that he might interact with some House members on the bill. A high foreign affairs support score was coded as favorable to this measure.[5]

A cross-pressure theory of voting has been discussed in election research (Lazarsfeld, Berelson, and Gaudet, 1944; Campbell, Converse, Miller, and Stokes, 1960; Pool, Abelson, and Popkin, 1965). However, it has never been elaborated fully for legislative voting:

> Representatives subject to conflicting pressures must be able to balance these pressures, decide which ones are more important, or attempt to please all by casting conflicting votes on a succession of roll calls. In some cases, on the other hand, a congressman with conflicting pressures may be more free than others to exercise independent judgment (Turner, 1951a, p. 165).

> When section and party pull in different directions on an issue the representative faces a difficult situation which may result in a qualified attitude. But when section and party both pull in the same direction the legislator has every reason to take an extreme position far in that direction (Grassmuck, 1952, pp. 123–124).

> When two senators from the same state belong to the same party, they tend to identify with similar groups, and to have similar voting records. When they are of different parties, their electoral followings may be radically different even though contained within the confines of the same state (Matthews, 1960, p. 233).

The simulation model of legislative voting treats the components and variables discussed in terms of a simple cross-pressure mechanism.

Lane (1965, p. 198) has noted that, "three major conflict situations may exist on the basis of the *direction* of the [political] identifications." In the first situation, a person is drawn by two or more positive attractions, in the second, he is repelled by two or more positions, and in the third, a position is equally attractive and repellent.

Where pressures do not conflict but rather converge, individuals tend to make decisions earlier (Lazarsfeld, Berelson, and Gaudet, 1948). Our simulation model is designed so that many representatives with reinforcing pressures will have their vote determined at the individual stage of the model without entering the communication phase.

[5] The actual coding for each bill is presented in Chapters 5 and 7.

An example of this would be the case in which party and constituency both support the same vote decision. Vote decisions of congressmen subjected to any of the types of cross-pressures Lane noted are likely to be postponed until legislator interactions have been simulated.

On the basis of these notions, the propositions that have been built into the model are:

Proposition 42:   When pressures salient to political decision-making are convergent, decisions tend to be made earlier than when salient pressures conflict (Lazarsfeld, Berelson, and Gaudet, 1948, p. 64; Campbell, Converse, Miller, and Stokes, 1960, pp. 81–82).

Proposition 43:   Persons with intense preferences who make early voting decisions are more likely to be influencers and those who postpone voting decisions tend to be targets of influence.

As mentioned previously research on legislative behavior has not been systematically evaluated nor has a theory of voting been developed that encompasses cross-pressure theory. Notions of conflicting pressures impinging upon legislative decisions are found throughout the literature, however, including Dexter (1965), Bailey (1950), and Wahlke, Eulau, Buchanan, and Ferguson (1962). The specific formulation of propositions concerning time of vote decisions and the separation and identification of influencers and influencees have been drawn from voting studies. Utilizing hypotheses from non-legislative research seems warranted because (1) voting decisions are involved in both cases—one concerning presidential elections and the other roll-call votes, and (2) the propositions are of a low theoretical level, minimizing error related to transference between different political situations. The research of Routt (1938) and Patterson (1959), among others, provide convincing arguments that interpersonal interaction is an important element of legislative policy-making. In the absence of well-developed propositions based on the study of legislatures, it seems appropriate to construct the model on the basis of propositions explaining political behavior in situations exhibiting a high degree of structural similarity to legislative voting decisions. This design strategy, of course, is evaluated by testing the performance of the communication phase of the model.

Operationalizing Relationships

In discussing *Computer Simulation Techniques* (1966), Naylor, Balintfy, Burdick, and Chu, note that one of the crucial questions concerning design is: "Have the estimates of the parameters of the system's operating characteristics been estimated properly?" (p. 37). In examining this question we see that up to this point our objective has been to identify relevant important variables and posit relationships among them. It has been pointed out that party affiliation, constituency characteristics, personal ideology, length of service, committee assignment and other factors are related to roll-call votes. Our present problem is to evaluate and weigh the importance of these variables and their interrelationships in determining the vote decisions.

It is conceded that party affiliation is the most important factor in the explanation of legislative roll calls. On the surface this might indicate that party should be given greater weight than other variables. Setting the parameters for the impinging variables in this manner is not satisfactory, however, for two reasons. First, legislative research reported in Chapter 1 indicates that the importance for all the relevant variables, including party, is specific to the issue. Second, the research assigned importance to these variables by applying statistical analyses to large numbers of roll calls. Thus, for any given subset of roll calls within any given study, such as those conducted by Turner (1951), Truman (1959), or MacRae (1958), the explanatory power of a given variable, such as party or constituency, might fluctuate considerably. This is due to statistical averaging involved in summarizing roll-call voting across a number of issues. One goal of our present model is to simulate the votes of individual legislators on specific roll calls as well as to simulate the behavior of groups of legislators across issue dimensions. For these reasons, each variable in the individual stage of the model was assigned a unit value of one.

Parameter estimation in simulation models often must be made in an arbitrary fashion and because of this, predictive power and representativeness must be sacrificed. The model cannot exceed the theoretical richness or precision of the research and data base. As with grouping constituency attributes into ordinal categories, so it is with assigning parameter weights of unitary value to predisposition factors, sacrifices must be made in constructing a specific model from empirical research and verbal theory. The extent of these sacrifices, however, can be estimated only after the performance of the model has been evaluated.

In general, each time a given characteristic of a roll call matches the corresponding characteristic of a congressman, he is disposed to vote for it. If the representative is a Democrat and the bill is introduced by a Democratic administration he is favorably disposed toward it. In cases where a political characteristic of a roll call does not match that of a given congressman, he is opposed to it.

The simulation model uses simple numerical values to represent salient audiences (MacRae, 1958) or cues (Truman, 1959) as they affect congressmen confronting roll calls. The initial voting predisposition of each congressman toward each bill is set at zero (0). The variables of party, region, state, committee, minority reporters, and party leaders are weighted equally with respect to creating a predisposition score. If the party dimension of the bill matches that of the congressman, the predisposition changes from zero (0) to plus one (+1). On the other hand, if the party dimension of the roll call and the congressman do not match, the predisposition score changes from zero (0) to minus one (−1). A predisposition score with a plus value disposes the representative to vote yes on the roll call; a minus value disposes the legislator to vote no. Some variables alter the predisposition score more than one unit. The sponsor of the bill is given a weight of plus two (+2), competitive constituencies are weighted two (2) whereas safe districts are weighted one (1), and representatives with extreme ideology scores are predisposed plus or minus two (±2).[6]

After every coding dimension characterizing a roll call is matched against the corresponding characteristic of a representative, the net predisposition is calculated. The final predisposition score is important for two reasons: (1) it provides a basis for dividing representatives between those whose votes are determined and those whose votes are undetermined, and (2) it provides greater influence for those with large predisposition scores in the communication stage.

---

[6] The cut-off points for calculating memory weights are: below 15% or above 85% the weight is two, between 15% and 35% and between 65% and 85% the weight is one, and between 35% and 65% the weight is zero. These percentages are calculated by dividing the total number of votes into the number of times each representative has supported the administration. The algebraic sign is determined by whether the vote supports or opposes the policy of the administration.

The cut-off parameter, dividing representatives into decideds and undecideds, is based on a net predisposition score of plus or minus two (± 2). Thus when a net predisposition score of two salient dimensions is pushing a congressman toward a particular vote, he enters the communication process as an influencer. Those with predispositions of either minus one (-1), zero (0), or plus one ($+1$) enter the communication stage as targets of influence. Figure 4 depicts the general flow chart of the individual stage of the model.

A large predisposition score has two implications for interactions in our simulated legislature. First, it means that a given representative has an intense, definite position on an issue. For example, this might be the case in which a rural Republican was opposed to a Democratic program for urban development. Second, it means that a given legislator will have more influence because his interpersonal interactions will be intensified. Thus legislator A with a predisposition of plus five ($+5$) will have more influence than legislator B with a minus two (-2), when they both approach legislator C with a predisposition score of zero (0). As a result of the calculations in the computer model, the predisposition score of an undecided representative will move one-half of the distance from his original predisposition score to the average of the predisposition scores of the members they contact.

Non-Voting

The simulation model does not provide for non-voting because of (1) the accidental factors involved and (2) the lack of attention given to this aspect of Congressional behavior in the research literature. Only congressmen in the simulation corresponding to those actually voting on a particular roll call are included in the analysis of simulation output.

Outputs of the Individual Stage as Inputs to the Communication Process

As a roll call enters the communication stage it is characterized by a distribution of congressional support, opposition, and ambivalence. This distribution of Congressional predisposition scores provides the content for communications among legislators. A significant body of legislative research and theory would be excluded if a model of legislative voting failed to include interpersonal interactions. Legislative policy is not determined solely by the effect of impersonal variables on each representative (Routt, 1938; Fiellin, 1962; Patterson, 1959).

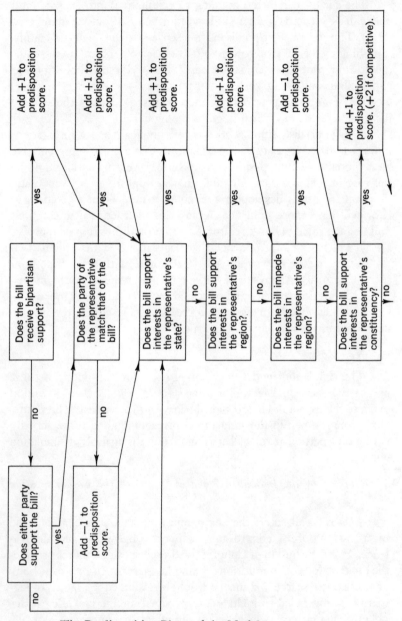

FIGURE 4. The Predisposition Phase of the Model

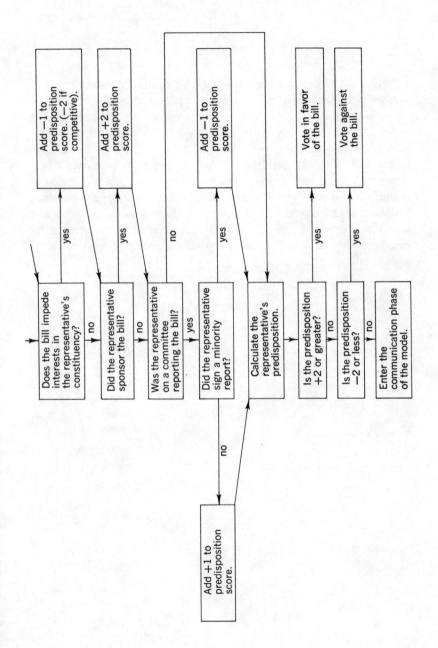

Summary

The individual stage of the simulation model identifies each congressman and each roll call by a set of variables related to legislative decision-making. The variables defining a roll call are matched against those defining congressmen, and identify which congressmen are subjected to cross-pressure on a measure and which congressmen have salient audiences who reinforce them. All representatives with a predisposition score more or less than zero become influencers in the communication process. Those confronting a roll call that has little salience for them or that subjects them to cross-pressures so that they do not satisfy the parameter cut-off, enter the communication phase as undecideds and are subject to influence from congressmen with more intense predispositions.

Simulating
Communication and Influence
in the House

In this chapter, we turn to a consideration of the second phase of our simulation model. This phase represents an attempt to build a theoretical representation of the communication and influence process in the House. Because of the relative paucity of empirical studies on the communication network in the House and because of the number of alternative communication networks that could develop with respect to a given topic of discussion, the structure of this phase of the model differs from that of the deterministic additive predisposition phase.

AN OVERVIEW OF THE MODELING STRATEGY

Stochastic Process

Although the predisposition phase of the model is deterministic, the communication phase involves a stochastic process. In this process

The materials of Chapters 4, 5, and 6 appeared in part in Michael J. Shapiro, "The House and the Federal Role: A Computer Simulation of Roll-call Voting," *The American Political Science Review*, June, 1968.

each representative's conversation partners are chosen on a probabilistic basis. The use of a stochastic process in a simulation model is one of a number of types of abstractions that can be made (Chorufas, 1964, p. 21). Stochastic processes suggest themselves as suitable abstractions in two instances, when the comparable process in the referent system is stochastic, and when the information available as to the determinants of the observed outcomes in the referent system is limited.

Our use of a stochastic communication process is predicated on both of these situations. The actual communication process in the House is stochastic in the sense that the conversation partners of a given representative from one bill to the next depend, in part, upon chance encounters. Our knowledge of those representatives who actually do hold conversations is limited. We have, however, information about the number of conversations the average representative has and about the types of representatives who hold conversations, and it is on the basis of this type of information that we have attempted to represent the communication process in the House.

Sampling

Because a stochastic process is involved, the operation of our model requires samples within a sample to be taken. The model as a whole can be looked upon as a sample, for, as Orcutt has pointed out, the components included in a model are probability samples of the components that would be included in more extensive conceptual models of the system (1962, p. 99). Our stochastic process involves sampling in that the components of that process for each operation of the model, and the conversation partners of each representative that enters the process, constitute a sample of the components that would be obtained from repeated operation of the model—the entire membership of the House.

Self-Contained Versus Nonself-Contained Models

A self-contained model generates outputs and predicts inputs, once it is started, without additional inputs having to be administered (Orcutt, Greenberger, Korbel, and Rivlin, 1961, p. 23). Our model of roll-call voting in the House is non self-contained as its continuous operation requires that a bill be entered for each step of the model. However, the model is self-contained for the purpose of processing one bill, for the inputs necessary for the operation of the communication process are generated as outputs of the predisposition phase.

Aggregate Versus Systemic Approaches

As Abelson (1966) has pointed out, the simulation gap between a machine and a group is greater than the gap between a machine and an individual. The problem in social process simulations is where to locate the control of the group. On the one hand there is the aggregative approach in which each individual in the simulation makes his responses in turn, and on the other, the systemic approach in which no autonomous processes within individuals are included. In both the predisposition and communication phases of our model the aggregative approach is employed. Predispositions are calculated independently for each representative in the predisposition phase, and each representative carries his predisposition into the communication phase as a determinant of the amount of influence he may exert or receive in confrontations with other representatives.

Prognostic Versus Process Simulations

Simulations have been characterized as prognostic and process simulations (Abelson, 1962; Abelson and Bernstein, 1963). Both of these types are concerned with projection forward in time. The distinction is that while a prognostic simulation is exclusively concerned with the specification of future outcomes (Pool, Abelson, and Popkin, 1964 and 1965), a process simulation is concerned with certain aspects of the processes leading up to future outcomes as well as the outcomes themselves. Our simulation is thus a process simulation in that, in addition to our concern with the prediction (or better postdiction) of voting outcomes in the House, we are concerned with illuminating the processes that lead up to the roll-call results that occur.

THE COMMUNICATION PROCESS: THE ELEMENTS OF THE MODEL

We now turn to a specification of the communication process. This part of our simulation model is included because it enhances the performance of the model and examines the interpersonal relations among representatives which we have hypothesized to be important determinants of their roll-call voting behavior.

There are, as we have indicated, three basic elements of a computer simulation model: components, variables, and relationships (Orcutt, 1960, p. 898). The basic components in both phases of our model are the individual representatives in the Eighty-eighth Congress. The input variables in the communication phase of our model are the predispositions generated for each representative in the predisposition phase. The status variables are those attributes chosen to describe each representative: his party, state, region, constituency attributes, committee and leadership positions, and seniority. The output variables are the predispositions that result after the communication process for one bill is completed. The relationships in the communication phase specify the structure and operation of this process. The propositions upon which that structure and operation are based are expressed operationally as instructions programmed for the computer.

The Inputs

Not all the representatives are influenced during the communication phase of the model on each bill, but all representatives are potential influencers. Each representative's potential influence over his colleagues on a given bill is a function of the predisposition that he develops during his confrontation with the bill during the predisposition phase. Only those representatives whose predispositions fall between the plus two and minus two range enter the communication process to be influenced. The others' final votes are determined in the predisposition phase.

The decisions on who enters the communication phase are based upon propositions from both social-psychological findings of influence and conformity in groups in general, and findings related specifically to the influence on representatives' voting behavior. From the former we get:

Proposition 44:   Individuals with more extreme attitude positions are less susceptible to influence than individuals with less extreme attitude positions (Hovland, Harvey, and Sherif, 1957).

From the latter we get:

Proposition 45:   A legislator with two or more pressures such as party and constituency influencing his vote in the same direction is unlikely to be susceptible to further influence concerning his vote (Turner, 1951, p. 125).

The decisions involved when a representative approaches the communication phase of the model are depicted in the flow chart in Figure 5. For the sake of simplicity, we have assumed that the communication process for all legislators is based upon the predispositions derived before the process is begun. No cycling of the process is carried out to take account of the possibility of a diffusion of influence in which predispositions generated as a result of communications among representatives become the basis for further influence in later communicative interactions.

The Status Variables[1]

Bauer, Dexter, and Pool have asserted that, "the U. S. House of Representatives is above all a communication node which serves to unify a large and heterogeneous land by bringing into confrontation a group of men representing its various parts" (1964, p. 445). It has been observed, on the other hand, that the patterns of interaction in legislative bodies tend to reinforce rather than moderate basic cleavages (Wahlke, Eulau, Buchanan, and Ferguson, 1962, p. 224). In constructing our communication process we have attempted, based upon investigations of interactions in legislative bodies, to simulate the types of confrontations that a legislator is likely to engage in when, because of either a lack of significant cues or a conflict among them, he has not evinced a strong predisposition to vote for or against a given bill.

The method employed to simulate these confrontations is an adaptation of the method of "pseudo partners" that Abelson and Bernstein used in their fluoridation referenda simulation (1963). With this technique, they matched conversation partners on the basis of potentiality for conversation, which was calculated as a function of social network information, a meshing of demographic characteristics and shared habitual loci of discussions about community issues. They based their conversation rates upon the levels of interest in the issue under discussion. We have adapted this procedure to the social network in the House by basing our conversation partner matching decisions on knowledge of the structure and processes of legislative systems in general and the House in particular.

The variables we have chosen to represent the structure of the

---

[1] "Status" here refers to the structure of the process being modeled.

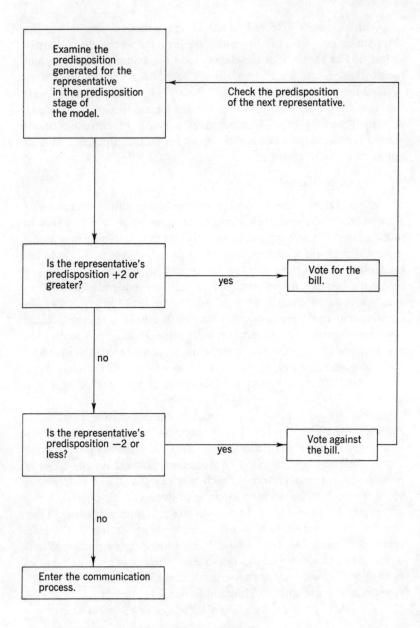

FIGURE 5. The Communication Entry Criteria

communication network in the House are based upon observations of the frequency of interactions between representatives with attributes of their conversation partners, and the general observations that representatives seek information from certain types of colleagues, and, finally, that some representatives, particularly those in positions of leadership, seek to give information or exert influence on certain types of bills. For the purposes of communication, then, each representative is described in terms of his party, state, region, constituency characteristics, leadership positions, committee memberships, rank on each committee, and seniority.

The Relationships

The first determination made when a representative enters the communication process is whether or not he has a conversation with the president. Such a conversation could be, for the sake of simplicity, a conversation either with the president or one of his legislative liaisons. Including the president in the communication process is predicated on the observation that presidential-legislative relations of this type have been institutionalized in the postwar period (Neustadt, 1955).

Proposition 46: The president communicates with legislators in order to influence the passage of his legislative programs.

As is indicated in the flow chart of Figure 6, we have confined the president's communications with representatives to cases in which legislation that is a part of his program is concerned.

The probabilities of conversation generated when the president confronts a representative are depicted in Figure 6. To arrive at these probabilities we begin by setting a limit on the average number of representatives that the president might confront on bills that are a part of his program. Here we assume that his number of contacts would approximate the number of contacts of the formal leaders of the majority party in the House—speaker, majority leader, and whip. After setting a limit (approximately 45 contacts) we can apportion his contacts so that the total number on a given bill will approximate our limit. For these approximations we assume that his frequencies of interaction with the various types of representatives is similar to those of a representative. Thus, he is given more contacts with the members

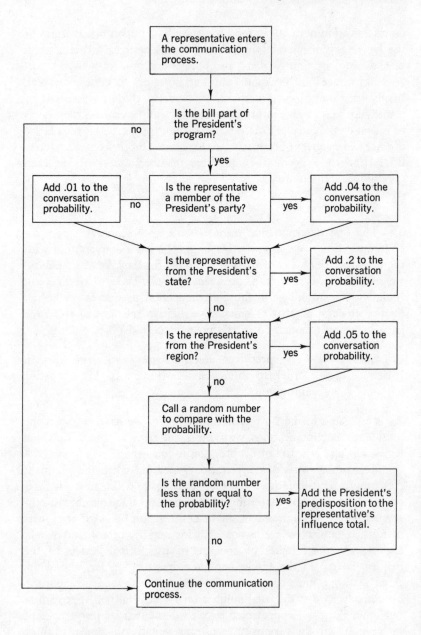

<small></small>

FIGURE 6. Communication with the President

of his party, representatives from his home state, and representatives from his region of the country.

Proposition 47: The president communicates more frequently with members of his own party than with opposition party members.

Proposition 48: The president communicates more frequently with representatives from his home state than with other representatives.

Proposition 49: The president communicates more frequently with representatives from his region than with other representatives.

When the probability of conversation between the representative and the president is calculated, a random number is called. If the random number is less than or equal to that probability, it is assumed that a conversation took place and the president's predisposition on the bill (plus two if he favors the bill and minus two if he opposes it) is added to the influence total for that representative.

The representative then enters that part of the communication process in which it is decided with which members of the House he will converse. In this part of the process he confronts all 434 of his colleagues. For each confrontation a probability of conversation is calculated, based on a matching of attributes of the representative and his potential influencers. As in the case of confrontations with the president, a random number is called after each of these confrontations. This number is compared with the probability of conversation generated, and, when it is less than or equal to that probability, results in the addition of the predisposition that the conversation partner developed in the predisposition phase of the model to the representative's influence total.

The formal leadership of the House is prominent in the communication process because as Truman has observed, "The House has four and one half times as many members as the Senate. From this schoolboy fact comes the tendency for the formal leadership in the House to correspond closely to the actual . . ." (1959, p. 145). Thus in the first part of the matching process (shown in the flow chart in Figure 7) it is determined whether the representative entering the communication process is an elected leader. If he is, it is then deter-

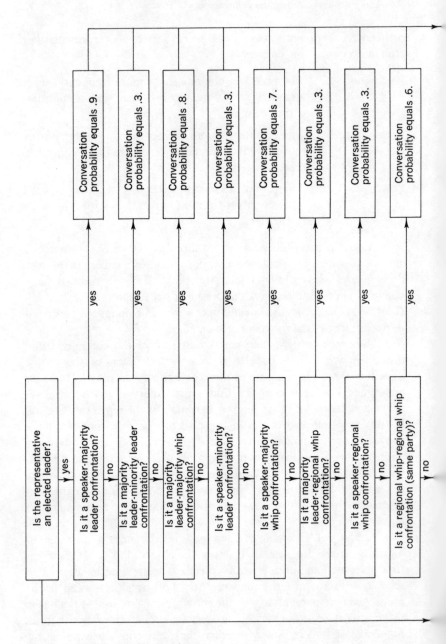

FIGURE 7. Leadership Interactions

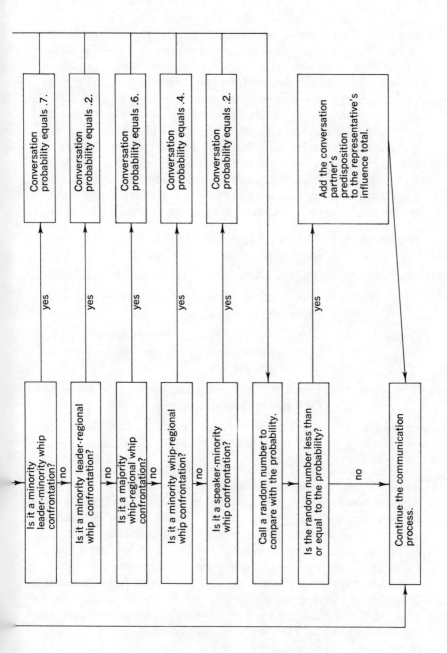

mined whether or not his potential conversation partner is an elected leader. This flow chart indicates the probabilities of conversation generated when the various types of leadership confrontations take place. These probabilities are derived from the general observation that the leadership in the House interacts frequently, and from the findings of investigations of state legislative bodies which indicate that the presiding officer (speaker) and majority leader have a close relationship and that the interactions between these two and the minority leaders are somewhat less frequent (Wahlke, Eulau, Buchanan and Ferguson, 1962, p. 225). These probabilities are based, in addition, on the finding that frequent interactions occur between the whips and whip organizations, and between these and the other elected leaders (Ripley, 1964).

Proposition 50:   The formal leadership in the House tends to correspond closely to the actual leadership.

Proposition 51:   The leadership in the House interacts frequently.

Proposition 52:   The speaker of the House and the House majority leader consult each other frequently.

Proposition 53:   The relationship between the speaker and majority leader is closer than that between either of them and the minority leaders.

Proposition 54:   Frequent interactions occur between the whips and the whip organizations.

Proposition 55:   Frequent interactions occur between the whips, whip organizations and other elected leaders.

The probabilities of conversation among the legislative leaders are based, in part, on the average total number of communications in which a non-leader becomes involved in legislative bodies. To distinguish formal elected leaders, we made use of the finding that the leaders become involved in twice as many communicative interactions on the whole as do the rank and file members of legislative bodies (Wahlke, Eulau, Buchanan, and Ferguson, 1962, p. 226). The probabilities that appear in Figure 4 are thus based upon an extrapolation from the total number of communications in which leaders become involved. The relative apportioning of probabilities for inter-party as opposed to intra-party confrontations is explicated in our discussion of non-leadership interactions below.

Proposition 56:   House leaders are involved in twice as many communicative interactions as rank and file members.

The flow chart in Figure 8 depicts the beginning of that part of
the communication phase in which a representative who holds no positions of elected leadership becomes involved after having confronted
the president. The first determination made in this section is whether
the potential conversation partner is a regional whip assigned to the
region of the representative. The high probability of conversation generated when the representative confronts his regional whip is based
upon the finding that such a conversation actually does take place on
most bills (Ripley, 1964).

Proposition 57:   A representative is contacted by his regional whip
before most roll calls.

The next set of determinations depicted in Figure 8 constitutes the
matching of attributes between the representative and his potential
conversation partner. Like the other types of confrontations discussed,
the probabilities of conversation generated are based on the limit set
for the average total number of communications in which a representative tends to become involved. That average falls between 25 and
30 and is derived from investigations of communicative interactions
in legislative bodies. It has been found that in general legislators in state
legislative bodies exert personal influence over approximately a dozen
colleagues (Wahlke, Eulau, Buchanan and Ferguson, 1962, p. 222).
We have added another half dozen to take account of the larger size
of the House which increases the possibility of a wider acquaintance-
ship, and the remainder has been added to represent the communications that a representative has with both elected and seniority leaders
in the process of carrying out the task of legislating (Truman, 1959,
pp. 145–275).

Proposition 58:   Representatives speak to an average of 25 to 30
colleagues before a roll call.

The apportioning of the probabilities for confrontations between
representatives involves a matching procedure. This procedure begins
with a determination of whether the representative and his potential
conversation partner are members of the same party. The relative size
of the probabilities for inter- and intra-party interactions is based on

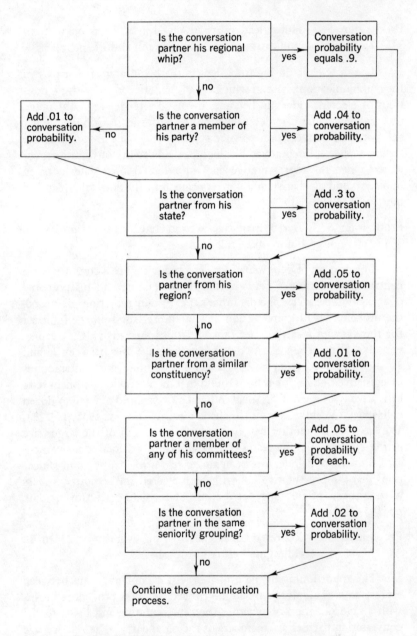

FIGURE 8. Rank and File Interactions

the finding that a representative tends to have four times as many communicative interactions with members of his own party as with members of the opposition (Routt, 1938, p. 135; Wahlke, Eulau, Buchanan, and Ferguson, 1962, p. 224).

Proposition 59:   A representative tends to have four times as many communicative interactions with members of his own party as with members of the opposition.

The matching procedure continues with a determination of whether the representative and his potential conversation partner are from the same state delegation. The additional probability of conversation added for intra-state confrontations is based upon the observation that state delegations in legislatures are somewhat cohesive in their voting behavior (Matthews, 1960, p. 231; Truman, 1959, p. 253; Kessel, 1964; Froman and Ripley, 1965, p. 62) and upon legislators' reports that their state delegations are important sources of their communications about legislation (Ross, 1965). The size of the probability relates, again, to the limit set for the total number of communications a legislator can be expected to have and is weighted on the basis of inferences drawn from the above sources as to the importance of the state delegation as opposed to other factors in the communication process.

Proposition 60:   State delegations are important sources of communication for representatives.

The next determination is whether the representative and his potential conversation partner come from the same region. The probability of conversation added for intra-regional confrontations is based upon both observations of interactions in legislative bodies (Routt, 1938, p. 135; Patterson, 1959, p. 103) and reports of conversation frequencies by members of the House (Ross, 1965). The probability is also based on the limit set for total communications.

Proposition 61:   Representatives communicate disproportionately with colleagues from their region.

The next matching determination depicted in the flow chart of Figure 8 is whether the representative and his potential conversation partner represent similar constituencies in terms of their urban-rural attributes. The probability of conversation that is added for a confrontation between representatives with like constituencies is based upon the two findings, that those with similar constituencies engage in a greater than average number of communications (Fiellin, 1962, p. 78), and that there is a slight tendency for those with similar constituencies to demonstrate cohesion on roll-call votes in the House (Truman, 1959, p. 210).

Proposition 62:   Similarity of constituency is a source of communication among representatives.

Committee membership is the next matching determination for confrontations. The probability of conversation that is added when the confrontation is between representatives who share a committee assignment is based, first of all, on the common sense supposition that those who share committee assignments will have some communications in the course of carrying out those assignments, and secondly on the finding that those sharing committee assignments in the House demonstrate a slightly greater than average cohesiveness on roll-call votes (Truman, 1959, p. 277).

Proposition 63:   Representatives communicate with colleagues who share their committee assignments.

The last matching determination relates to the effect of shared seniority status on communicative interactions of representatives. The probability of conversation added for shared seniority status is based upon the finding that interactions in legislatures occur disproportionately within seniority groupings (Wahlke, Eulau, Buchanan, and Ferguson, 1962, p. 224; Routt, 1938, p. 135).

Proposition 64:   Communication among representatives takes place disproportionately within seniority groupings.

In addition to all these criteria, the probabilities of conversation for these and other types of confrontations are based upon the two findings that representatives in the majority party are more cohesive on roll-call votes than those in the minority party (Truman, 1959, p. 286), and that more interactions take place between members of the majority party (see Proposition 25, p. 38). The use of this criterion can be noted particularly in the apportioning of probabilities of conversation for interaction between leaders and rank and file representatives to be described.

The flow chart in Figure 9 depicts the determinants of communication that are included to account for interactions between rank and file representatives on the one hand, and, on the other, the seniority leaders and technical experts in the House, who are the chairmen and members of the committees through which the bill that is the subject of communications passes. The probabilities of conversation that are added for these confrontations are apportioned on the basis of a matching of party between the representative and his potential conversation

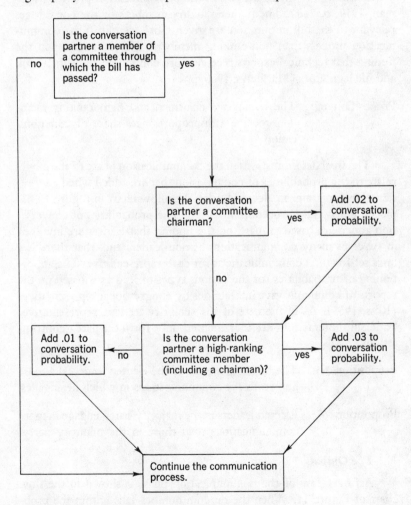

FIGURE 9. Interactions with the Seniority Leaders

partner. It is assumed that the representative seeking technical advice on bills will show biases similar to those displayed in his choices of other conversation partners. In keeping with the finding that the seniority leaders (committee chairmen) are especially cohesive with their party on bills that have gone through their committees, the chairmen are weighted more heavily in the communication process (Truman, 1959, p. 240). The higher ranking members of the committees relevant to the bill in question are given more weight in the communication process than non-ranking members. This is based upon the finding that technical experts receive more communications than rank and file legislators (Matthews, 1960, p. 252).

Proposition 65:   The committee chairmen and high ranking members receive a disproportionate share of communication.

The final determinations in the communication phase of the model relate to the probabilities of conversation that are added when a representative confronts an elected leader. The flow chart in Figure 10 depicts the matching procedure involved. The probabilities of conversation added are based, in part, on the finding that leaders are involved in twice as many communications as non-leaders and, that there is a limit set for total communications for each representative. The apportioning of probabilities for the various types of leaders is based on the reports of communicative interactions by congressional representatives (Ross, 1965). As in the case of the seniority leaders, representative-leadership interactions are incremented only for intra-party confrontations.

Proposition 66:   The higher the rank of the elected leader, the more numerous the communications in which he engages.

Proposition 67:   Elected leaders in the majority party engage in more communications than those in the minority party.

The Outputs

An overview of the communication phase is shown in the flow chart of Figure 11. When the random number falls within the probability of conversation calculated for a given confrontation, the predisposition of the conversation partner is added to the influenced

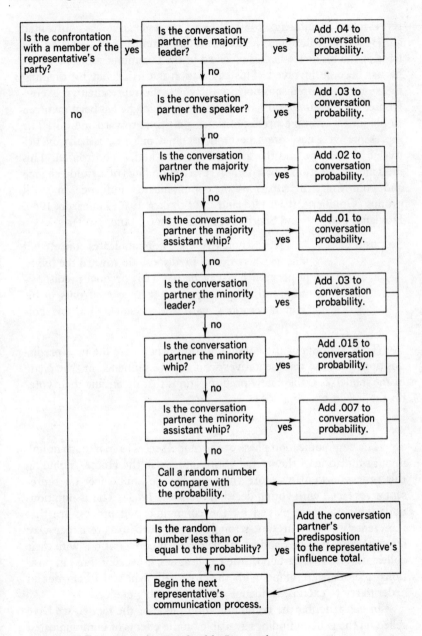

FIGURE 10. Representative-Leadership Interactions

representative's influence total. When a representative has confronted all 434 of his colleagues, his new predisposition is calculated on the basis of the influence he has received in the communications in which he has become involved. This calculation is carried out by dividing the sum of the predispositions with which the representative is confronted by the number of conversations in which he has been involved to obtain the average predisposition or attitude toward the bill. The representative's new predisposition becomes one that is halfway between his old one and the average one that he has confronted. This influence calculation is based upon research findings of attitude change and conformity in situations of communicated influence in small groups (Goldberg, 1954; Hovland and Pritzker, 1957; Zimbardo, 1960; Hovland, Harvey, and Sherif, 1957; Fisher and Lubin, 1958).

Proposition 68:   A representative who communicates on a bill changes his original predisposition toward the bill to a position halfway between his original predisposition and the average one that he confronts in his communications with the president and his colleagues.

Thus, outputs of the communication process are the new predispositions of those representatives who receive influence in that phase of the model. It is these new predispositions that determine their votes on the bill in question.

Conclusion

The communication phase of the model serves as an important link in our simulation of the overall voting process in the House. Including this process articulates more fully the "inside" influences on representatives faced with voting decisions (Polsby, 1963). The assumptions underlying the part played by the communication process are that representatives who are not strongly predisposed to vote either way on a given bill will seek additional cues in their conversations with their colleagues and that certain of their colleagues, especially those in positions of leadership, along with the president, will seek them out in order to try to exercise influence over their voting choices.

In constructing the communication phase of the model, we have relied on the general findings available on the effects of communicated influence on attitudes and on the more specific findings with respect

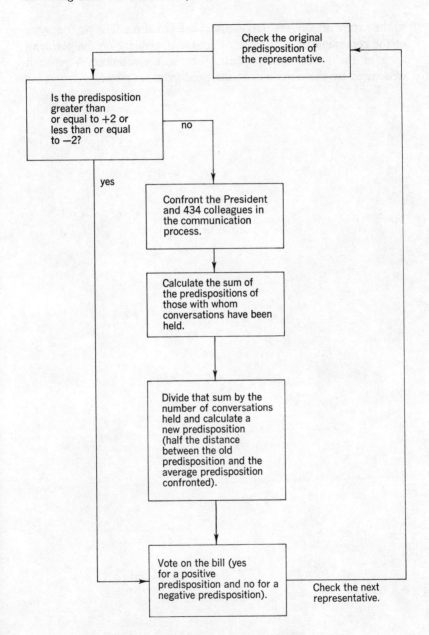

FIGURE 11. An Overview of the Communication Phase

to the nature of conversation partners in legislatures. The performance of the communication phase is, of course, dependent on the performance of the predisposition phase, for the communication phase is structured by the outcomes of the predisposition phase.

5

The House
and the Federal Role:
Simulating
Roll-Call Voting

Since 1945 much of the U. S. Congress' work has involved issues concerning the size and scope of activities of the federal government. The legislation in this area can be traced, for the most part, to measures which originated during the period of the New Deal in response to the Great Depression, and to measures enacted during World War II to meet the short-run exigencies attendant to rapid economic and social mobilization. From the viewpoint of an expanding federal role, the Eisenhower years are of some moment. While they marked a lull in the expansionist trend carried out under the Democratic presidencies of Roosevelt and Truman, their significance is that despite the change in administration, there was no redress of the policies begun under Roosevelt. While most of the Republican legislators were on record as opposing federal expansion, the failure of the Republican party to introduce and enact legislation to reverse this trend resulted in a new plateau of federal activity and congressional debate which carried into the Kennedy and Johnson administrations.

Although the Eighty-seventh Congress, which met during Kennedy's first two years in the White House, did not enact the quantity of legislation which could expand the federal role in the way Kennedy had called for in his inaugural address, during the Eighty-eighth Congress both parties supported a larger federal role than they had previously. The voting behavior of the first session of the Eighty-eighth Congress concerning the federal role has been summed up as follows: "At no time in 1963 did the majority of both parties reject a larger federal role" (*Congressional Quarterly Almanac*, 1963, p. 724). The statement holds true, with two exceptions, for the second session in 1964. Here, we shall report the results of the processing of 21 bills dealing with the federal role in our computer simulation model of roll-call voting in the Eighty-eighth session of the U. S. House of Representatives.

SIMULATING VOTING ON THE FEDERAL ROLE IN THE HOUSE

The bills chosen for our simulation of House voting on the federal role are essentially the same as those identified by the Congressional Quarterly Service pertaining to this issue. A few recommittal motions on these bills have been added to provide a larger number of bills for the purpose of analysis, and to allow for comparisons between bills introduced by the Democratic administration and those introduced by Republicans (the latter having been reflected, for the most part, in recommital motions). Because the bills are the inputs for our simulation model, the substantive issues with which they are concerned will be discussed in connection with the explication of the coding of the bills for input.

It is the coding decisions made on each bill that serve to shape the nature of the input of both the predisposition and communication phases of our simulation model. The coding is undertaken in the context of the theoretical basis of the model as a whole and provides an important link in the theory building process—the specification of the nature of the subject matter to which the propositions built into the theoretical model are thought to apply. We now turn to that specification, the coding of the individual bills.

ROLL-CALL VOTES ON THE FEDERAL ROLE

Federal Aid to Education

Viewing the cleavages that have developed in the Congress over legislation dealing with the federal role in education, Munger and

Fenno have found that, "although individual congressmen may occasionally support a particular formula or principle against constituency interest, the greater number have treated the issue as one in which their responsibility is to serve as delegates protecting their constituents' welfare" (1962, p. 36). Thus such issues as flat grants versus equalization (the former supported by those with wealthy constituents and the latter by those with poorer ones), the inclusion of parochial schools in aid programs, and the inclusion of funds for racially segregated facilities have tended to manifest themselves in cleavages on roll-call votes dealing with the federal role in education.

The coding of the seven education bills processed in our simulation model is shown in Table 1.[1] It can be noted that these bills are of two basic types: substantive issues and recommittal motions. All of the recommittal motions represent Republican attempts to block passage of administration bills. They are coded 2 in the party column to indicate Republican sponsorship. All of the substantive bills are administration bills and are coded 1 in the party column of two of the bills to indicate Democratic sponsorship and 3 in the party column of one bill (HR 4955) to indicate bipartisan support for the administration bill.

With the exception of the recommittal motion on HR 4955, only the administration sponsored bills, which are addressed to substantive aspects of the federal role, receive regional and constituency coding. The recommittal motion on HR 4955 is coded with a 2 in the percent Negro constituency column and a 12 in the region column to indicate Negro support and southern opposition to the motion which was prompted by feelings that an anti-segregation clause should be included in HR 4955.

The first substantive bill, HR 12, was a proposal to furnish funds that would match grants given for constructing teaching facilities for medical schools and issuing loans to medical students. This bill is coded 2 in the rural farm and rural non-farm constituency columns because the bill was proposed to help overcome the shortages of medical help in rural areas. The next substantive education bill, HR 4955, a vocational educational bill designed to update an existing program is coded 3 in the urban constituency column because the need for vocational ed-

---

[1] It should be noted that the size of the numbers in the coding scheme has no weighting significance. They are chosen arbitrarily for purposes of classification to be recognized by the computer, not to indicate the relative contribution of the variables. These parameters have been explicated in Chapter 3.

TABLE 1. The Coding of the Education Bills

	HR 12	HR 12*	HR 4955	HR 4955*	HR 4955*	HR 6143	S 3060*
Party	1	2	3	2	2	1	2
State							
Region					12	12	
Constituency (percentage)							
Urban			3				
Rural Non-Farm	2						
Rural Farm	2						
Negro					2		
Foreign Stock							
Own Occ H'sing							
White Collar						2	
Plurality							
Competitiveness							
Committees	11		11			06	
Minority Reports	097 083ᵇ					054,011 241,373,119	
Sponsorship	170	097		030	030	152	147
President							
Party	1	1	1	1	1	1	1
State	21	21	21	21	43	21	
Region	1	1	1	1	2	1	2
Federal Role	1	2	1	2	2	1	2

* denotes recommittal motions

ᵇ Three digit numbers are identifications for individual representatives who sponsored bills or signed minority reports.

Coding Index

PARTY	REGION	CONSTITUENCY
Democrat 1	South (against) 12	High Urban 3
Republican 2		High Rural Non-Farm 2
Bipartisan 3		High Rural Farm 2
		High White Collar 2

(Continued at bottom of opposite page)

ucation is felt primarily in urban areas. The administration's higher education bill, HR 6143, which embodies a five year program for federal grants and loans for constructing facilities for higher education is coded for both region and constituency. It is coded 12 in the region column to indicate southern opposition because supporters of the bill suggested withholding funds from facilities that are racially segregated, and it is coded 2 in the white collar constituency column because the aid is apportioned on the basis of the number of high school graduates per capita.

All the substantive bills can also be distinguished by the coding of committees which reported the bills out, the House Interstate and Foreign Commerce Committee in two cases (HR 12 and HR 4955) and the House Education and Labor Committee in one (HR 6143). In the cases where committee is coded on a bill, additional codes may be included which indicate the identification numbers of those members of the committee who signed the minority report. These can be noted for two members of the Interstate and Foreign Commerce Committee on HR 12 and five members of the Education and Labor Committee on HR 6143.

Additional identification coding indicates the individual sponsors of the bills and motions. Sponsors coded on the education bills included Representative Harris on HR 12 (#170), Representative Green on HR 6143 (#152), Representative Devine on the HR 12 recommittal motion (#097), Representative Bell on the two HR 4955 recommittal motions (#030), and Representative Goodell (#147) on S 3060.

The final coding on all seven bills relates to the president's position and the implications of each bill for the expansion or diminution of the federal role. President Kennedy is coded 1 21 1 on the three substantive bills and one of the recommittal motions on HR 4955. He took

---

COMMITTEES
    Interstate and Foreign Commerce 11   FEDERAL ROLE
    Education and Labor 06   Expansion 1
                                           Diminution 2

PRESIDENT
    Party   Region
        Democrat 1   East 1
    State   South 2
        Massachusetts 21
        Texas 43

a position in favor of the three bills and against the recommittal motion. The first 1 indicates his party (Democratic), 21 stands for his home state (Massachusetts), and the last 1 his region of the country (East). President Johnson took a position opposing the other recommittal motion on HR 4955 and is coded 1 43 2. The 1 indicates his party (Democratic), 43 his home state (Texas), and 2 his region of the country (South).[2] The coding relating to the federal role is dichotomous. When a 1 is coded in the federal role column, as is the case for all four administration bills, it means that the bill involves the expansion of the federal role. When a 2 is coded in that column, as in the case of the four Republican sponsored recommittal motions, it indicates that the bill involves the diminution of the federal role. This code is in keeping with the designation of the Congressional Quarterly Service for these bills and serves to relate the bills to the memory of past votes that is a part of the predisposition phase of the simulation model.[3]

The Federal Role in Agriculture

Pennock, in his roll-call analysis of the effects of party and constituency on postwar price support legislation, found that despite a general agreement by both parties on the need for a federal price support policy, there has been a major divergence over whether such supports should be rigid or flexible, the Republicans favoring the former and the Democrats the latter. While party polarization has been a significant factor in agricultural price support roll-calls, as in the case of the education bills, the effects of constituency can be discerned. Senators and representatives who have been "cross-pressured" in that their rigid versus flexible stand has conflicted with the interests of their constituents have followed constituency more frequently than party (Pennock, 1956, p. 168).

The coding of the four bills dealing with the federal role in agriculture is indicated in Table 2. Three bills, the cotton subsidy bill, HR 6196, the wheat-cotton bill, an extension of HR 6196, and a food stamp bill, HR 10222, part of the wheat-cotton package, are administration

---

[2] The functions of the coding of the president's position are explicated in the discussion of the communication phase of the model in Chapter 4.

[3] All of the coding decisions are based upon the discussion of the bills in the *Congressional Quarterly Almanac* for 1963 and 1964. The criteria for coding that are described are explicit to the extent that a reliability check with a naive coder yielded a coefficient of 1.00.

bills and as such are coded 1 in the party column to indicate Democratic sponsorship. The recommittal motion on the cotton subsidy is coded 2 in the party column because it is a Republican sponsored motion. Like the education bills, the three substantive bills demand expansion of the federal role and so are coded 1 in the federal role column. The Republican sponsored recommittal motion is coded with a 2 as a sign to keep down the federal role.

TABLE 2. The Coding of the Agriculture Bills

	HR 6196 cotton	HR 6196*	HR 6196 wheat cotton	HR 10222
Party	1	2	1	1
State				
Region				
Constituency (percentage)				
Urban				
Rural Non-Farm				
Rural Farm				
Negro				
Foreign Stock				
Own Occ H'sing				
White Collar				1
Plurality				
Competitiveness				
Committees	01		01	01
Minority Reports	087,029,183, 254[b],387,314, 361,247,225, 174,119,100, 028,192		087,029, 183,254, 387,314, 361,247, 225,174, 119,100, 028,192	087,029, 183,254, 387,314, 361,247, 225,174, 119,100, 028,192
Sponsorship	079	183		

TABLE 2. *(Continued)*

	HR 6196 cotton	HR 6196*	HR 6196 wheat cotton	HR 10222
President				
Party	1	1	1	1
State	43	43	43	43
Region	2	2	2	2
Federal Role	1	2	1	1

* denotes a recommittal motion

b Three digit numbers are identifications for individual representatives who sponsored bills or signed minority reports.

Coding Index

PARTY
   Democrat 1
   Republican 2

CONSTITUENCY
   Low White Collar 1

COMMITTEE
   Agriculture 01

FEDERAL ROLE
   Expansion 1
   Diminution 2

PRESIDENT
   Party   Region
     Democrat 1   South 2
   State
     Texas 43

The only substantive coding in the case of the agriculture bills is a 1 code in the percent white collar constituency column for the food stamp bill indicating a positive response from representatives with low white collar districts. This would be expected because the bill was designed to increase the food buying power of low income families. There did not seem to be any consensus on regional or constituency benefits to accrue from the cotton and wheat-cotton bills, such that substantive coding would be warranted. All three of the substantive bills are coded for the House agriculture committee (01) as they were all reported out of that committee.

Finally, a number of individual representatives including the president are coded as taking positions on the bills. Fourteen members of the Agriculture Committee signed the minority report for the three substantive bills. Their identification numbers appeared in the minority report columns to indicate their positions against the bills. President Johnson, who supported the three substantive bills and opposed the recommittal motion, is coded 1 43 2 as a Democratic, Texan, southern president for the purposes of his role in the communication process. Representatives Cooley (079) and Hoeven (183) are identified as sponsors of the cotton subsidy bill and its recommittal motion respectively.

The Federal Role in the Cities

In addition to the vocational education bill, six roll-call votes in the Eighty-eighth Congress were concerned with federal involvement in urban areas. This represents part of a trend of the federal government toward increasing involvement in the cities. Roscoe Martin noted that the period from 1932 to 1963 saw a dramatic rise in federal payments directly to local governments, a major portion of which found its way into urban areas (1965, Chapter 5).

The coding of the six federal-city bills processed in our simulation model is indicated in Table 3. Administration bills are coded 1 in the party column to indicate Democratic sponsorship. They are the Kennedy administration air pollution bill, HR 6518, the Johnson administration library service bill, S 2265, the urban mass transportation bill, HR 3881, and the anti-poverty bill, HR 11377. The Johnson administration housing bill HR 12175 is coded 3 in the party column to indicate bipartisan support, and a recommittal motion on the library services bill is coded 2 in the party column to indicate Republican sponsorship.

The five substantive bills are coded 1 in the federal role column for they promote expansion, and the recommittal motion is coded 2 in that column indicating its diminution. Four of the five substantive bills are coded 3 in the urban constituency column because of the benefits they provide for urban areas. The air pollution bill was primarily directed toward the problem of urban smog, the library services bill was designed to extend a federal program stimulating library construction in urban areas, the urban mass transportation bill was designed to provide considerable federal assistance for urban mass transportation, and

TABLE 3. The Coding of Federal-City Relations Bills

	HR 6518	S 2265	S 2265*	HR 3881	HR 12175	HR 11377
Party	1	1	2	1	3	1
State						
Region				12		
Constituency (percentage)						
Urban	3	3		3	3	
Rural Non-Farm				7		
Rural Farm				7		
Negro						
Foreign Stock						
Own Occ H'sing						
White Collar						1
Plurality						
Competitiveness						
Committees	11	06		04	04	06
Minority Reports				039,173, 384,336, 045,211, 232		131,154,314, 147,054,011, 241,030,373, 119,384
Sponsorship			242			
President						
Party	1	1	1	1	1	1
State	21	43	43	43	43	43
Region	1	2	2	2	2	2
Federal Role	1	1	2	1	1	1

* denotes a recommittal motion

b Three digit numbers are identifications for individual representatives who sponsored bills or signed minority reports.

(*Continued at bottom of opposite page*)

the housing bill, an extension of FHA mortgage and insurance programs, included a program to provide for considerable urban renewal.

Additional substantive coding includes a 1 code in the white collar constituency column of the anti-poverty bill (because of its benefits to low income families) and regional and constituency codes on the urban mass transportation bill indicating opposition to a bill of this nature on the part of various rural and southern interests. Sevens are coded in the rural constituency columns to show that rural representatives maintained that the bill extended the federal government into an area that was already provided for by other federal programs. A 12 is coded in the region column to indicate opposition from southern representatives who expressed fear that funds would be withheld from segregated facilities.

Three committees were involved in reporting out the substantive bills and are so coded. The House Banking and Currency Committee (code 04) reported out the urban mass transportation and housing bills. The House Education and Labor Committee (code 06) reported out the library services and anti-poverty bills. The House Interstate and Foreign Commerce Committee (code 11) reported out the air pollution bill.

Finally, the president and individual representatives are coded as

---

Coding Index

PARTY	CONSTITUENCY	REGION
Democrat 1	High Urban 3	South (against) 12
Republican 2	High Rural Non-Farm (against) 7	
Bipartisan 3	High Rural Farm (against) 7	
	Low White Collar 1	

COMMITTEES	FEDERAL ROLE
Interstate and Foreign Commerce 11	Expansion 1
Banking and Currency 04	Diminution 2
Education and Labor 06	

PRESIDENT

Party	Region
Democrat 1	South 2
State	
Texas 43	

taking positions on the bills. President Kennedy is coded 1 21 1 as a Democratic, Massachusetts, eastern president for his support of the air pollution bill, and President Johnson is coded as 1 43 2 as a Democratic, Texan, southern president supporting the library services, urban mass transportation, anti-poverty, and housing bills. He is seen to oppose the recommittal motion on the library services bill. Seven members of the Banking and Currency Committee signed the minority report to indicate opposition to the urban mass transportation bill; 11 members of the Education and Labor Committee are seen as opposed to the anti-poverty bill for the same reason. Representative Martin (#242) is coded for his sponsorship of the recommittal motion on the library services bill.

The Federal Government and Due Process

The recent involvement of the federal courts in the area of civil liberties, in which they defined the jurisdiction of the states over the rights of individual citizens, provoked a reaction in the Eighty-eighth Congress. This reaction was both positive and negative as manifested by the passage of the civil rights and reapportionment bills respectively. The civil rights bill, HR 7152, reinforced the decisions of the courts by providing for federal involvement to guarantee citizens equality of voting rights, access to public accommodations, and education. However, the reapportionment bill, HR 11926, opposed the action of the courts by preventing them from interfering with the rights of the states to conduct their domestic political affairs.

The coding of the two bills is indicated in Table 4. Although the civil rights bill had the effect of expanding the federal role and the reapportionment bill succeeded in lessening it, neither of the bills is coded in terms of its relationship to the federal role, contrary to the designation of the Congressional Quarterly Service. This coding is omitted because they failed to fulfill the criteria of reproducity for items in a Guttman scale when scaled with the other 19 bills (Guttman, 1950).

The civil rights bill is coded 3 in the party column because it had bipartisan support. The reapportionment bill was not sponsored by either party and so is coded 4 in the party column. As the Texas state delegation sponsored this bill, 43 is coded in the state support columns. The substantive coding for the civil rights bill includes a 2 in the per-

TABLE 4. The Coding of the Civil Rights, Reapportionment, Mental Retardation, and Communications Regulation Bills

	HR 7152	HR 11926	S 1576	HR 8316
Party	3	4	3	3
State		43		
Region	12			
Constituency (percentage)				
Urban		8		
Rural Non-Farm		2		
Rural Farm		2		
Negro	2			
Foreign Stock				
Own Occ H'sing				
White Collar				
Plurality				
Competitiveness				
Committees	12, 16	12, 16	11	11
Minority Reports	371,077,397, 111[a]	038,092,237,293		070,424,128, 398,013,308, 082,363,377, 235,322,275, 099,180,404
Sponsorship				334
President				
Party	1		1	
State	43		21	
Region	2		1	
Federal Role			1	2

[a] Three digit numbers are identifications for individual representatives who sponsored bills or signed recommittal motions.

(Continued at bottom of the next page)

cent Negro constituency column to indicate support from representatives from constituencies with a large percentage of Negroes (except for southerners), and a 12 code in the region columns to indicate opposition from southern representatives. The substantive coding of the reapportionment bill reflects the urban-rural conflict. The rural constituency columns are coded with a 2 to indicate rural support and the urban constituency column is coded 8 to indicate urban opposition to the bill.

Both the Judiciary and Rules Committees are coded for both bills (12 and 16 respectively) as they reported them out. The Rules Committee is included in these cases because of its substantial involvement in the substantive aspects of the bills. Seven members of the committees involved in the civil rights case and four in the reapportionment case signed minority reports and are identified in opposition to the bills. President Johnson is coded in the usual manner as supporting the civil rights bill. He took no position on the reapportionment bill.

Bipartisanship: Mental Health and Communications Regulation

The two remaining bills processed in our simulation model, a mental retardation bill, S 1576, and a communications regulation bill, HR 8316, are two of the four federal role roll calls in the Eighty-eighth

---

Coding Index

PARTY
    Bipartisan 3
    No Party Relevance 4

STATE
    Texas 43

REGION
    South (against) 12

CONSTITUENCY
    High Negro 2
    High Urban (against) 8
    High Rural Non-Farm 2
    High Rural Farm 2

COMMITTEES
    Judiciary 12
    Rules 16
    Interstate and Foreign Commerce 11

PRESIDENT
    Party   State
        Democrat 1   Massachusetts 21
                Texas 43

FEDERAL ROLE
    Expansion 1
    Diminution 2

Region
    East 1
    South 2

Congress that received bipartisan support. The passage of the mental retardation bill resulted in an expansion of the federal role while the passage of the communications regulation bill resulted in its diminution.

The two bills are coded in Table 4. Both bills are coded 3 in the party column indicating their bipartisan support. The mental health bill which provides federal aid for construction of community health centers, university and state clinics for the mentally ill, and centers for research into the causes of mental illness is coded 1 in the federal role column to indicate that it involves federal expansion. However, the communications regulation bill was introduced to prohibit the FCC from setting standards governing the length and frequency of radio and television commercials without the approval of the Congress and is coded 2 in the federal role column indicating a diminution of the federal role.

The House Interstate and Foreign Commerce Committee is coded in both cases as it reported both bills out. President Johnson is coded as supporting the mental retardation bill. He took no position on the communications regulation bill. Finally, eight members are identified in the minority report column of the communications bill and Representative Rogers is identified (#334) for his sponsorship.

THE PERFORMANCE OF THE SIMULATION MODEL

Because our simulation model aggregates the voting choices of each individual representative to obtain roll-call results, the basic evaluation of the model's performance has been carried out at both the macro and micro levels. The former involves the extent to which the voting outcomes in the simulation approximate the actual voting outcomes in the Eighty-eighth Congress, and the latter considers the extent to which each individual representative's voting behavior in the Congress is approximated by his voting behavior in the simulation.

Considering, first of all, the macro level, or voting outcomes as a whole, Table 5 shows the simulated and actual voting outcomes. In the simulation, the splits in the votes tend to be larger than were the splits in the actual votes. The average split in the simulated votes is 141 while the actual split was 109. This difference can be explained in terms of the types of representatives for which the model's performance is below its overall average for individual voting performances. We will talk about the sources of error in our discussion of the micro level performance of the model. Despite this tendency for the simulation to over-emphasize the splits in the votes, the correct outcomes are obtained by the simulation for all the bills. Using the splits in the simulated and actual votes as raw scores, we obtain a product-moment coefficient of correlation between the simulated and actual voting outcomes of .97.[4] While this suggests a very positive evaluation of the simulation model, the assessment of the model's performance must be made in the context of the kinds of performances that are obtained with variations or alternative formulations of the model.

Before turning to this type of assessment, we should consider the micro level performance of the original model. The percentages of individuals voting the same way in the simulation as they actually voted are presented for each bill in Table 5. The average percentage of individuals correctly simulated across the 21 bills is 84. Breaking down that figure for the three different categories of party sponsorship, we find that for the four bipartisan bills the average percentage of individual representatives correctly simulated is 89. The percentages obtained for the 11 Democratic administration bills and the six Republican sponsored recommittal motions are 82 and 85 respectively. The assessment of these differences and all others reported must take account of the amount of variation in results that can be obtained because of the stochastic variation of the communication phase of the model.[5]

The percentages for the three party sponsorship categories are explained in terms of the types of individuals for which the simulation performs best. The most significant difference is between Democrats and Republicans. Averaging the percentages across all the bills yields scores of 86 and 79 for correctly simulated Democratic and Republican

---

[4] If the sums of yes votes and no votes are used as raw scores instead of the splits between the yeses and nos on each vote, the correlation coefficients become .95 and .96 respectively. It must be noted that the systematic difference in the size of the splits between actual and simulated votes results in a slight exaggeration of the model's performance with the correlation coefficient because this statistic controls for differences in the range of the scores for the two variables.

[5] To determine this variation two bills were run ten times each, one being a bill with a large number of representatives entering the communication phase and the other relatively few. In each case, the amount of variation in the percentage of representatives did not exceed 1 percent. Thus any difference in percentages, that is 2 percent or greater, can be treated as an actual difference.

TABLE 5. The Actual and Simulated Voting Outcomes

Bill	Simulated Voting	Percent Correct	Actual Voting
HR 12 (*recommittal*)	171-239	84	171-239
HR 12	280-128	77	288-122
HR 4955 (*recommittal*)	153-244	92	181-217
HR 4955	382-13	92	378-27
HR 6143	294-104	70	287-113
S 1576	353-3	94	335-18
HR 6196 (*recommittal*)	167-237	81	179-224
HR 6196	232-168	78	216-182
HR 6518	262-119	82	273-109
HR 4955 (*recommittal*)	159-214	90	180-193
S 2265 (*recommittal*)	153-209	86	174-188
S 2265	241-121	76	254-107
HR 7152	323-100	84	290-130
HR 8316	362-0	87	317-43
HR 10222	245-173	90	229-189
HR 6196	238-175	89	211-203
HR 3881	230-172	82	212-189
HR 11377	247-172	85	226-185
HR 12175	371-3	82	308-68
HR 11926	221-170	78	218-175
S 3060 (*recommittal*)	148-197	76	107-237

representatives respectively. All of this difference is accounted for by bills sponsored during the Democratic administration, for representatives in both parties voted correctly in the simulation an average of 83 percent on the Republican sponsored recommittal motions and an average of 85 percent on the four bills with bipartisan support. The simulation thus tends to over-emphasize the cohesiveness of the Republicans on Democratic sponsored bills despite the attempt to build greater cohesiveness for Democrats than Republicans into the communication phase of the simulation model.[6] It may be that it is this poorer micro level performance of the simulation for Republican representatives that accounts for part of the lower percentage of correctly simulated representatives on Democratic sponsored bills.

Turning to the regional breakdown of the extent to which individual representatives are correctly simulated, we find that the poorest performance for regions is exhibited by the southern representatives with an average percentage correct for the 21 bills of 78. The next lowest percentage correct is from the eastern representatives at 83. The midwest, mountain, and far western representatives are simulated correctly with percentages of 88, 86, and 86 respectively.

It would appear that our simulation model confronts the same difficulty as the Democratic whip organization, predicting the voting behavior of the southern delegation (Froman and Ripley, 1965). Because of the difficulty of discerning those bills on which the conservative coalition of Republicans and southern Democrats takes shape, we must code the southerners as regular Democrats which will predispose them with respect to party affiliation, in the same manner as the other Democratic representatives. By so doing, we miss a sizable percentage of their vote on occasions when they side with Republicans against "liberal legislation" such as bills proposing the expansion of the federal role. It is undoubtedly the incorrect simulating of the voting of some southern representatives that accounts, in part, for the greater average split in the simulated votes as opposed to the actual votes, for the switching over of southerners has the effect of moderating the heavily party oriented cleavages which account for the larger splits in the simulation.

The slightly lower average percentage obtained for eastern representatives can probably be explained in terms of the traditional liberalism of eastern representatives. Several eastern Republican representatives usually side with the Democrats on liberal legislation, and in

[6] In keeping with previous research, the structure of our communication process provides for more communicative interactions within the majority party.

general, eastern representatives from both parties tend to have more liberal voting records than their colleagues from other parts of the country. Our simulated voting results on the communications regulation bill, HR 8316, illustrate this phenomenon quite clearly. Coding the bill as a bipartisan measure resulted in an average percentage of representatives correctly simulated of 87. Because this bill resulted in the diminution of the federal role, however, a number of liberal easterners who had voted against the bill ended up for it in the simulation as a result of the bipartisan effect. Thus, a below average percentage of eastern representatives of 84 was obtained. Again, this slightly lower performance for eastern representatives would have the effect of overemphasizing the voting splits as is the case of the performance on southern representatives.

Looking at the performance of the simulation model for the different representatives in terms of the types of constituencies they represent reveals a range of correctly simulated individual representatives from 86 percent for representatives with predominantly urban constituencies to 81 percent for representatives with predominantly rural non-farm constituencies. The representatives with mainly rural non-farm constituencies were correctly simulated on an average of 82. These differences are probably a result of the distribution of Republicans and southern Democrats in terms of constituency types. A disproportionate share of non-southern Democrats represent constituencies with a high proportion of urban residence while Republicans and southern Democrats disproportionately represent rural farm and non-farm constituencies.

One interesting type of constituency variation in percent correctly simulated is for competitive versus non-competitive districts. Representatives from the former were simulated correctly on an average of 85 percent while those from the latter were simulated correctly on an average of 83 percent.[7] While this can be interpreted as evidence of the relatively stronger hold that the parties (the strongest determinant in our model) have over representatives who are less firmly established, the fact that competitive districts are not equally allocated on a regional or party basis confounds the clear interpretation of this result.

[7] These percentages are computed across only those 12 bills on which constituency effects are coded.

In considering a categorization of representatives that is related to the competitiveness of constituencies we can look at the extent to which the voting behavior of representatives with different seniority positions are correctly simulated. The findings from legislative research suggest that representatives with high seniority rankings are less likely to be loyal to their party and are less predictable in terms of their roll-call voting (Garceau and Silverman, 1954; Truman, 1959; Matthews, 1960). The results of the simulation tend to support this proposition. Our simulation yields an average percent of 87 for the low seniority members of the House, while the average percent obtained for representatives with high seniority standing is 82. Again, this finding must be assessed in the context of possible confounding factors, not the least of which is the fact that southern representatives possess a disproportionate share of the high seniority positions in the House.

Summary

Now, we have seen that the model can simulate the voting on federal role issues in the Eighty-eighth Congress with results that quite closely match the outcomes of the actual voting at both the macro and micro levels. We have also gained some insights as to how far the voting behaviors of different types of representatives can be explained in terms of our theoretical formulation of the voting process.

The Validity of
the Simulation Model:
Alternative Formulations on
Federal Role Votes

Pool, Abelson, and Popkin have commented upon the problems inherent in evaluating a complex simulation model. They state:

> A complex model can predict real-world outcomes and yet be wrong in many details. It may predict accurately because the main effects are correctly represented and yet the model may contain many irrelevances. So one must always question the details of a complex model, even if it passes the test of good prediction (1964, p. 64).

Simulation is a modeling strategy that is, perhaps, ideally suited for questioning the details of a model. Assumptions can be changed, and in a matter of minutes the data can be processed on the reformulated model. This chapter shall consider the details of our simulation model of roll-call voting in the House in order to examine the validity of the model as it was originally formulated, and to test the sensitivity of the determinants or effects programmed into the model which represent those processes and propositions that we had deemed to be significant factors in roll-call behavior.

THE PARTY EFFECT

There is little doubt that on the American legislative scene, party is the most significant factor in roll-call voting cleavages. Recent quantitative analyses of roll-call voting in the Congress have explored this phenomenon (among others) systematically (Turner, 1951; MacRae, 1958; Truman, 1959; Froman, 1963). Because party is a prominent determinant in our simulation model, appearing as both a predisposing factor and a communications parameter, a systematic assessment of the performance of the model requires the consideration of the extent to which the party's effect contributes to that performance.

We examine, first of all, the performance of a simulation model in which party is the only effect. If we maintain the same coding rules for party sponsorship and omit all other determinants we get the voting results shown in Table 6. The actual results and the results obtained with the original model are also shown for purposes of comparison. Using the voting splits as raw scores, we obtain a product-moment coefficient of correlation between the actual voting splits and the just party simulated voting splits of .80 as compared with the .97 coefficient obtained between the original model and the actual voting results. The micro level performance or average percentage of representatives correctly simulated by the just party model is 78 as compared with the 84 percent obtained with the original model. It is clear that party plays an important role in the performance of the simulation model, but it is also evident that the remaining effects built into our model are not irrelevant, for the results obtained with only the party effect are not as good as those obtained with the original model at either level.

Another way to assess both the model and the effect of the party variable is to run the model in its original form without including the party effect. When this is done the performance criteria are markedly similar to those obtained when just party is used to simulate the voting. The voting results obtained with this variation of the model are presented in Table 7 along with the results obtained with the just party model and the actual votes for purposes of comparison. The product-

TABLE 6. The Results of the "Just Party" Model

Bill	Original Model	Percent Correct	Party Model	Percent Correct	Actual Voting
HR 12 (*recommittal*)	171-239	84	171-239	84	171-239
HR 12	280-128	77	240-170	77	288-122
HR 4955 (*recommittal*)	153-244	92	163-235	93	181-217
HR 4955	382-13	92	399-0	95	378-27
HR 6143	294-104	70	237-163	60	287-113
S 1576	353-3	94	357-0	95	335-18
HR 6196 (*recommittal*)	167-237	81	169-235	81	179-224
HR 6196	232-168	78	232-168	78	216-182
HR 6518	262-119	82	220-163	78	273-109
HR 4955 (*recommittal*)	159-214	90	160-213	90	180-193
S 2265 (*recommittal*)	153-209	86	153-209	86	174-188
S 2265	241-121	76	210-152	74	254-107
HR 7152	323-100	84	423-0	69	290-130
HR 8316	362-0	87	362-0	87	317-43
HR 10222	245-173	90	242-176	90	229-189
HR 6196	238-175	89	237-177	89	211-203
HR 3881	230-172	82	235-167	75	212-189
HR 11377	247-172	85	245-167	84	226-185
HR 12175	371-3	82	374-0	81	308-68
HR 11926	221-170	78	0-0	00	218-175
S 3060 (*recommittal*)	148-197	76	148-197	76	107-237

TABLE 7. The Results of the "Just Party" and "Without Party" Models

Bill	"Just Party" Model	Percent Correct	Actual Voting	"Without Model Party"	Percent Correct
HR 12 (*recommittal*)	171-239	84	171-239	158-250	84
HR 12	240-170	77	288-122	353-55	78
HR 4955 (*recommittal*)	163-235	93	181-217	120-175	83
HR 4955	399-0	95	378-27	285-113	70
HR 6143	237-163	60	287-113	301-96	82
S 1576	357-0	95	335-18	272-83	75
HR 6196 (*recommittal*)	169-235	81	179-224	127-272	75
HR 6196	232-168	78	216-182	257-137	76
HR 6518	220-163	78	273-109	315-66	80
HR 4955 (*recommittal*)	160-213	90	180-193	121-243	84
S 2265 (*recommittal*)	153-209	86	174-188	171-188	88
S 2265	210-152	74	254-107	288-72	75
HR 7152	423-0	69	290-130	165-243	64
HR 8316	362-0	87	317-43	265-97	75
HR 10222	242-176	90	229-189	265-149	87
HR 6196	237-177	89	211-203	247-164	86
HR 3881	235-167	75	212-189	209-190	85
HR 11377	245-167	84	226-185	255-156	86
HR 12175	374-0	81	308-68	297-75	79
HR 11926	0-0	00	218-175	224-170	79
S 3060 (*recommittal*)	148-197	76	107-237	130-213	79

moment coefficient of correlation between the actual voting splits and those obtained with party removed from the model is .68, somewhat lower than that obtained with just party as the model. But the average percentage of representatives correctly simulated is 78, the same figure obtained for the just party simulation.

Two types of interpretations arise when we test the model's sensitivity with the party effect as the object subject of our manipulations. The relatively similar performance of the model with just party and without party suggests that the original model is somewhat overdetermined in terms of party. The absence of party in the second reformulation of the model is partly compensated because of the extent to which the communications process is structured by a party effect. This suggests that there may be a party surrogate in this prior phase that accounts for the similar performances.

The other types of interpretation afforded by our manipulation of the party effect relates to the types of issues processed in the model. Included in Table 7 along with the juxtaposed voting results of the just party and without party simulations are the percentages of representatives correctly simulated on each bill. If we examine separately the three different categories of party sponsorship—bipartisan, Democratic, and Republican—we can determine the extent to which the party effect is significant in each. These are broken down into the party sponsorship categories in Table 8.

First, considering the bills coded as bipartisan, we obtain an average percentage of correctly simulated representatives of 90 with the

TABLE 8. Comparison of the Original "Just Party" and "Without Party" Models on Three Party Sponsorship Categories

	Original Model Percent Correct	"Just Party" Model Percent Correct	"Without Party" Model Percent Correct
Bipartisan Bills	89	90	75
Republican Sponsorship	85	85	71
Democratic Sponsorship	82	70	79

just party model. This result is slightly better than the 89 percent obtained over the same bills with the original model. The percentage obtained with the without party model is only 75, which is considerably lower. Similarly, we obtain an average percentage of correctly simulated representatives on the Republican sponsored recommittal motions of 85. In the just party model this same figure is obtained with the original model. The percentage of 71 obtained with the without party model is, again, considerably lower.

When we examine the 11 remaining Democratic administration bills, however, we find that the percentage of correctly simulated representatives is only 70 for the just party model whereas the figure obtained with the original model was 82. The without party model, on the other hand, correctly simulates an average of 79 percent of the representatives on these bills. This reversal in performances between the party only and without party models suggests some validity for our presupposition about treating recommittal motions as incidents of party conflict rather than mediating the party effect with substantive coding for region and constituency variables as in the case of the Democratic administration bills. At a general level, this result tends to validate the inclusion of constituency and regional effects in the model, for these enhance its performance. To assess the regional and constituency effects more critically, however, we must directly manipulate them with further sensitivity testing of the model.

THE CONSTITUENCY EFFECT

Investigations of the relationship between the demographic and political characteristics of constituencies and the roll-call behavior of their representatives have been extensive. The findings from these studies all point in the direction of such a relationship (Turner, 1951; MacRae, 1952; MacRae, 1958; Pennock, 1956; Froman, 1963). While these investigations have not systematically explored the constituency effect from issue to issue in terms of the extent to which different types of issues result in different degrees of constituency loyalty on the part of representatives, Miller and Stokes's recent investigation explored the effect in this manner (1963). They found that representatives tend to pay attention to the desires they think their constituents have as well as the desires they actually do have, particularly on domestic welfare legislation. The close similarity between the welfare legislation of the

TABLE 9. The Results of the "Without Constituency" Model

Bill	Original Model	Percent Correct	"Without Constituency" Model	Percent Correct	Actual Voting
HR 12 (*recommittal*)	171-239	84	170-239	84	171-239
HR 12	280-128	77	242-168	77	288-122
HR 4955 (*recommittal*)	153-244	92	149-249	91	181-217
HR 4955	382-13	92	380-17	91	378-27
HR 6143	294-104	70	169-230	66	287-113
S 1576	353-3	94	352-4	94	335-18
HR 6196 (*recommittal*)	167-237	81	168-236	81	179-224
HR 6196	232-168	78	233-166	78	216-182
HR 6518	262-119	82	224-159	79	273-109
HR 4955 (*recommittal*)	159-214	90	158-215	90	180-193
S 2265 (*recommittal*)	153-209	86	150-212	86	174-188
S 2265	241-121	76	213-149	74	254-107
HR 7152	323-100	84	297-126	88	290-130
HR 8316	362-0	87	362-0	87	317-43
HR 10222	245-173	90	243-175	90	229-189
HR 6196	238-175	89	238-176	88	211-203
HR 11377	230-172	82	236-166	76	212-189
HR 12175	247-172	85	245-167	84	226-185
HR 12175	371-3	82	351-20	83	308-68
HR 11926	221-170	78	317-0	42	218-175
S 3060 (*recommittal*)	148-197	76	147-198	76	107-237

Stokes and Miller study, and our bills dealing with the federal role formed the basis upon which the decision to code constituency effects was made.

In order to examine the validity of constituency coding and the specific coding decisions, we have run the model on our 21 bills without the constituency coding that had been included in the original run. The voting results obtained are presented in Table 9 along with the actual voting results and the voting results obtained with the original model for purposes of comparison. The coefficient of correlation between the actual splits and those resulting from the "without constituency" simulation is .80 as compared with the .97 coefficient obtained between the original model and the actual votes.[1] It would appear that the constituency effect is not an irrelevant part of the simulation model.

To examine the extent to which the specific constituency coding decisions were well advised, we consider the micro level performance of the model without the constituency coding. The average percentage of representatives correctly simulated on the 12 bills for which constituency was coded is 78 for the run with the without constituency model. This compares with an average of 85 percent obtained for the bills with the original model. While this is not conclusive evidence of the validity of the specific coding decisions made for the constituency effects, it argues strongly for that validity. It tends to validate the model and to support previous findings on the effect of constituency factors on legislative roll-call voting behavior.

THE REGION EFFECT

Sectionalism or regional cleavages in Congressional voting behavior have been found in many investigations (Roach, 1925; Grassmuck, 1951; Key, 1949). In our simulation of bills dealing with the federal role, only four bills were coded as having regional effects. All of these were coded to suggest a negative predisposition on the part of southern representatives.

To test how much regional coding aided in the performance of the

[1] When we compute the correlation between the actual splits and the without constituency splits across only the 12 bills on which constituency was originally coded we obtain a coefficient of .78, as compared with a .95 obtained with the original model for the same bills.

simulation model, we processed the 21 bills without the regional coding. The voting results obtained with this without region model are presented in Table 10 together with the actual results and those obtained with the original model. The product-moment coefficient of correlation between the splits on the actual bills and those resulting from the "without region" simulation is .89 as compared with the .97 coefficient obtained between the actual voting splits and those resulting from the original simulation model.[2] Thus, the regional coding substantially improves the performance of the simulation model even though only four bills are coded as subject to a regional effect.

To test how well informed our specific regional coding was, we may examine the micro level performance of the without region model. The average percentage of representatives correctly simulated with this variation of our original model is 77 as compared with an average of 83 correctly simulated with the original model for the four bills on which regional effects were coded. We thus have partial validation of our regional coding decisions. It would appear that the substantive provisions of our simulation model (including both constituency and regional effects) is an important part of the legislative process involved in roll call voting. The inclusion of these effects has aided the overall performance of the model at the macro level, and has provided better individual performance of the model on the bills for which coding makes the substantive provisions relevant.

THE MEMORY EFFECT

On all but two of our bills, memory is coded to indicate whether the bill constitutes the expansion or diminution of the federal role. Thus, each representative has his predisposition affected if his past votes on the federal role issue suggest a positive or negative attitude toward its expansion. To examine how important an effect memory is in our model, we have run the bills through the model without including the memory effect. The results of the without memory simulation are presented in Table 11 along with the actual and original simulation results.

[2] When we compute the correlation between the actual splits and the without region splits across only the four bills on which region was originally coded we obtain a coefficient of .62 as compared with .99 obtained with the original model for the same bills.

TABLE 10. The Results of the "Without Region" Model

Bill	Original Model	Percent Correct	"Without Region" Model	Percent Correct	Actual Voting
HR 12 (*recommittal*)	171-239	84	171-139	84	171-239
HR 12	280-128	77	287-123	75	288-122
HR 4955 (*recommittal*)	153-244	92	165-233	92	181-217
HR 4955	382-13	92	385-13	92	378-27
HR 6143	294-104	80	338-61	70	287-113
S 1576	353-3	94	354-3	94	335-18
HR 6196 (*recommittal*)	167-237	81	168-236	81	179-224
HR 6196	232-168	78	232-167	78	216-182
HR 6518	262-119	82	252-129	81	273-109
HR 4955 (*recommittal*)	159-214	90	159-213	90	180-193
S 2265 (*recommittal*)	153-209	86	154-208	86	174-188
S 2265	241-121	76	239-121	77	254-107
HR 7152	323-100	84	423-0	70	290-130
HR 8316	362-0	87	265-97	75	317-43
HR 10222	245-173	90	244-174	90	229-189
HR 6196	238-175	89	238-176	89	211-203
HR 3881	230-172	82	244-158	78	212-189
HR 11377	247-172	85	246-166	85	226-185
HR 12175	371-3	82	371-3	82	308-68
HR 11926	221-170	78	225-169	78	218-175
S 3060 (*recommittal*)	148-197	76	147-198	76	107-237

TABLE 11. The Results of the "Without Memory" Model

Bill	Original Model	Percent Correct	"Without Memory" Model	Percent Correct	Actual Voting
HR 12 (*recommittal*)	171-239	84	171-239	84	171-239
HR 12	280-128	77	336-72	71	288-122
HR 4955 (*recommittal*)	153-244	92	153-249	93	181-217
HR 4955	382-13	92	399-0	95	378-27
HR 6143	294-104	70	314-80	73	287-113
S 1576	353-3	94	357-0	95	335-18
HR 6196 (*recommittal*)	167-237	81	169-235	81	179-224
HR 6196	232-168	78	232-168	78	216-182
HR 6518	262-119	82	280-102	81	273-109
HR 4955 (*recommittal*)	159-214	90	160-213	90	180-193
S 2265 (*recommittal*)	153-209	86	166-196	83	174-188
S 2265	241-121	76	271-89	71	254-107
HR 7152	323-100	84	322-100	84	290-130
HR 8316	362-0	87	362-0	87	317-43
HR 10222	245-173	90	246-171	90	229-189
HR 6196	238-175	89	237-177	89	211-203
HR 3881	230-172	82	172-229	78	212-189
HR 11377	247-172	85	245-167	84	226-185
HR 12175	371-3	82	374-0	81	308-68
HR 11926	221-170	78	226-168	78	218-175
S 3060 (*recommittal*)	148-197	76	148-197	76	107-237

Looking at the macro level performance of the without memory model, we obtain a product-moment coefficient of correlation of .97. This is the same coefficient obtained with the original model. The lack of memory's contribution can be further highlighted by viewing the results obtained when just memory is used to simulate the votes. The product-moment coefficient of correlation obtained between the actual voting splits and those resulting from the "just memory" simulation is only .21.

These findings suggest that the memory effect does not aid in the macro level performance of our simulation model. The presence of the memory effect may, however, account for the findings obtained when the party effect was manipulated. When we correlate the splits resulting from the just party simulation with those resulting from the just memory simulation we obtain a coefficient of .62. This suggests that memory tends to coincide, to some extent, with party membership and is thus somewhat of a party surrogate which may explain part of the similarity of the results obtained with the just party and without party simulations.

Despite memory's small role in the macro level performance of the simulation model, this performance of the without memory simulation model indicates that the memory effect is not entirely superfluous. The average percentage of representatives correctly simulated by the without memory model is 82 as compared with the 84 percent figure obtained when memory is included. The memory effect is a slight aid in the micro level performance of the model.

The performance of the memory effect on the different types of bills is of interest. Comparing the average percentage of correctly simulated representatives obtained with the without memory model with the original model for the four bipartisan bills, yields the same figure of 89. Similarly, the without memory model results in the same average percentage of representatives correctly simulated across the six Republican sponsored recommittal motions as in the original model, 85. On the Democratic administration bills, memory appears to aid the micro level performance of the model.

While the original model correctly simulated the voting behavior of 82 percent of the representatives on the Democratic administration bills, the without memory model correctly simulated only 79 percent of the representatives on these bills. Because it is these bills that deal with the substantive issues involved in legislation, the memory effect probably conveys the impact of ideological postures that have been found to have some effect on legislative roll-call behavior (Farris, 1958). In the case of recommittal motions and bipartisan bills, the content of the bill that tends to evoke ideological effects is obfuscated by party concerns and the bipartisan effect respectively.

THE COMMUNICATION EFFECT

We turn, finally, to a consideration of the contribution made by the communications phase of the model. Again, this assessment is made by testing the sensitivity of the effect by removing it. The voting results obtained when the model is run without the communications process are presented in Table 12 along with the actual and original simulation model voting results. Examining, first of all, the macro level performance of this alternative formulation of the model we obtain a product-moment coefficient of correlation between the actual voting splits and those resulting from the "without communications" simulation of .88 as compared with the .97 coefficient obtained between the actual and original model voting splits.

The micro level performance is also enhanced by the communication process. The average percentage of representatives correctly simulated by the without communications simulation model is 78 as compared with the 84 percent correctly simulated by the original model. Now we have a basis for believing that the communications process is not an irrelevant part of our overall model.

Several important questions can be raised with respect to internal aspects of the communications phase. In constructing the process, we found that changes in key mechanisms, such as the salience of the party effect, resulted in a diminution of the performance of the model as a whole. Changes in the average number of representatives' communications had similar effects on the model's performance. Although a thorough examination of the sensitivity of all the important effects in the communication process has not yet been conducted, the indications, thus far, suggest that the communications phase of our model is quite sensitive to changes in parameters and mechanisms.

Summary

So far, every alternative formulation of the model undertaken has decreased some aspect of the model's performance. This lends to the

TABLE 12. The Results of the "Without Communications" Model

Bill	Original Model	Percent Correct	"Without Communications" Model	Percent Correct	Actual Voting
HR 12 (*recommittal*)	171-239	84	173-222	84	171-239
HR 12	280-128	77	254-119	72	288-122
HR 4955 (*recommittal*)	153-244	92	155-233	90	181-217
HR 4955	382-13	92	303-34	74	378-27
HR 6143	294-104	70	188-133	62	287-113
S 1576	353-3	94	278-13	77	335-18
HR 6196 (*recommittal*)	167-237	81	170-221	79	179-224
HR 6196	232-168	78	220-168	78	216-182
HR 6518	262-119	82	219-120	76	273-109
HR 4955 (*recommittal*)	159-214	90	158-200	88	180-193
S 2265 (*recommittal*)	153-209	86	164-169	84	174-188
S 2265	241-121	76	207-121	72	254-107
HR 7152	323-100	84	298-100	83	290-130
HR 8316	362-0	87	265-96	68	317-43
HR 10222	245-173	90	237-170	89	229-189
HR 6196	238-175	89	226-176	87	211-203
HR 3881	230-172	82	169-177	77	212-189
HR 11377	247-172	85	228-168	85	226-185
HR 12175	371-3	82	285-25	74	308-68
HR 11926	221-170	78	214-167	77	218-175
S 3060 (*recommittal*)	148-197	76	147-183	76	107-237

evidence that the relatively good match obtained between the actual roll-call voting in the House on federal role issues and in our simulation is not a result of a number of errors or ill-advised hypotheses that cancel each other out to make the model right for the wrong reasons. What is especially significant is that a theoretical model, based upon propositions from legislative and face-to-face group research, can be used to simulate the roll-call voting on an issue area in two sessions of the House, with good performances at the macro and micro levels. To the extent that the model is successful in simulating roll-call voting on other issue areas, we may have confidence in its details and in its status as a theoretical overview of legislative voting.

The House
and Foreign Affairs:
Simulating
Roll-Call Voting

The House of Representatives helps to determine the strength and limits of foreign policy commitments through investigations, and through the authorization and appropriation of funds to support the international position of the administration. Whereas the Senate is instructed to "advise and consent" on international treaties and diplomatic appointments, the House is further removed from the planning of our foreign policy. The House has little power to initiate. Its business is to investigate, amend, and approve or disapprove of administration foreign policy proposals. Our simulation model of House voting will focus on approval or disapproval of administration proposals at the roll-call stage.

EMPIRICAL STUDIES OF FOREIGN AFFAIRS VOTING

Political scientists have long been interested in the study of foreign affairs policy-making, and have produced several investigations of congressional roll-call voting on foreign affairs issues. The roll-call vote has often been the dependent variable in these investigations. From this common basis, however, a variety of strategies have related personal, political, and demographic variables to these votes, and others have identified voting cliques using roll calls.

Grassmuck (1951) analyzed House and Senate roll calls for the period 1921 to 1941. He found that control of the executive was quite important for some foreign affairs issues:

> When Republicans occupied the White House, Republican senators and representatives were more defense-minded than Democratic legislators. When Democrat Franklin D. Roosevelt was "that man in the White House," Democratic congressmen championed military and naval appropriations while GOP delegates lagged behind (p. 32).

Grassmuck, however, also found consistent differences between the parties on aspects of foreign policy other than military and naval appropriations:

> During the twenties . . . the Democratic senators supported Republican presidents on the issue of international organization more than did Republican senators (p. 73).

Support of the foreign fiscal program was closely related to the party which controlled the presidency, and as fiscal programs became more important during the thirties, party acquired increasing importance on this issue.

Region was clearly related to foreign policy votes during this period:

> For sections having strong party ties, changes in administration meant considerable change in attitude. . . . Democratic party ties were reflected by the voting of southern congressmen who opposed army and navy bills to some degree in the twenties, then became quite favorable during the period of Democratic administration (p. 54).

To summarize the effects of region on foreign policy voting during the twenties and thirties: (1) the Northeast generally favored increased international participation supported by strong fighting forces, (2) the South tended to support foreign affairs policies that would bring success to the Democratic party and defeat to the GOP, (3) the Midwest did not take a strong stand against participation in permanent international organizations but opposed military and naval armaments, alliances, and entanglements, and (4) the West had no discernible regional position.

Constituency types were related to roll calls in that:

In the interwar period it was the district containing metropolitan population that elected a congressman who favored foreign loans and aid legislation. In counter fashion the legislator from the rural district often opposed such programs (p. 108).

This proposition held across party, section, and time, even though each of these factors weakened the relationship.

Turner's (1951) study did not focus primarily on foreign policy-making in Congress, but the time period of his investigation, 1930–1944, provides a nice overlap with the twenty-year span of Grassmuck's research. He found party cleavage on foreign affairs to be moderate and inconsistent because the parties tended to switch positions as control of the White House alternated. He noted, however, that:

The tendency for members of the majority party to support the administration and for the minority to attack it in foreign policy was only a tendency, and did not apply to all members (p. 56).

Turner found the Index of Party Likeness on substantive foreign policy issues (where 0 is complete party dissimilarity and 100 complete similarity) to be 68.4 for the four legislative sessions he investigated. He also found urban-rural conflict significant as this tended to support international action, and increased military, naval, and air appropriations. As far as sectional alignments on foreign affairs was concerned, "the most frequent source of conflict for West Central and other states in the Republican party was foreign affairs," (p. 155). The midwesterners were isolationists.

Dahl (1950) analyzed congressional voting on foreign affairs from 1933 to 1948. Before 1941, party cleavages were more important than sectional divisions; after 1941, party cleavage assumed less importance. Westerfield (1955) carried his study of foreign policy roll calls from the time of Pearl Harbor up to the Korean War. During this period there was significant regional variation in congressional voting on foreign affairs which was similar to the Grassmuck findings for the twenties and thirties. Northern Democrats gave more support to administration proposals than did Mountain and southern Democrats; this was especially true for party line votes (pp. 45–47). The Repub-

lican party found the "internationalist" Coastal regions opposed to the
Midwest (pp. 32–36). In the Democratic party, the Northeast, Midwest, and the Pacific Coast all supported the administration with an
average of slightly more than 90 percent (p. 45). Westerfield concluded that the presence of a Democratic administration seemed to
have the effect of holding party members together on foreign affairs,
which might have disintegrated under a Republican president (p. 46).

MacRae (1958) and Truman (1959) studied the Eighty-first
Congress. Roll-call votes were used to identify "dimensions of congressional voting" and voting blocs; in these cases foreign affairs was
only one of several areas of inquiry. Among Democratic representatives, MacRae found:

. . . the Rocky Mountain and Pacific representatives tended to be
more favorable to foreign aid, and the southern and rural borderstate
congressmen less favorable, than most of their northern urban colleagues
(p. 276).

Contrary to Grassmuck's finding, MacRae discovered no systematic
relationship between Guttman scale positions on foreign aid and
either urbanism or occupational status of the constituency within the
Democratic regional groupings (p. 276). In the Republican party,
foreign affairs scale positions were related to urban-rural divisions
within each region (p. 277). MacRae concluded that generally effects
of constituency were weaker on the "foreign-aid" scale than on other
(domestic) scales (p. 280).

Truman (1959) found that Republican members of the House
experienced higher disunity on foreign aid and foreign policy than did
Democrats (p. 149). This was consistent with his more general finding
that the minority legislative party was more fluid and flexible than the
majority (p. 281), because the Republicans in this Congress were the
minority party.

The importance of majority party status and the president's party
affiliation in producing congressional party cohesion on foreign affairs
was underlined by Kesselman (1961). A comparison of foreign aid
scales between the Eighty-first Congress, with a Democratic president,
and the Eighty-sixth Congress, with a Republican president, finds that
the Democrats shifted to a less internationalist position and the Republicans shifted to a more internationalist position. This relationship
should not be allowed to obscure the fact that a higher percentage of

congressional Democrats supported Eisenhower's foreign policy than did Republicans. Throughout the 1950's the Democrats continued to be the more internationalist of the two parties, control of the White House notwithstanding.

Farnsworth (1961) compared the Senate with its Foreign Relations Committee on selected foreign affairs roll calls. He found that members of the committee tended to be much more internationalist than did the Senate. In fact, members of the committee are apparently socialized by committee hearings and interaction with other committee members. They adopt more internationalist positions after serving on the committee.

. . . [the data] indicates that the committee in all five Congresses [from 1947–1957] underrepresented the anti-internationalist sentiment in the Senate (p. 173).

. . . newcomers tend to assume the attitudes already shared by the older committee members (p. 175).

. . . there is a noticeable decline in the number of anti-internationalist votes cast after each of these senators became members of the committee (p. 174).

One of the most recent and comprehensive investigations of foreign aid voting in the House was conducted by Rieselbach (1964). By looking at foreign aid roll calls from 1939 to 1958, he found the relationship between cleavage on the votes and party declining from an almost perfect association in 1939 to no statistically significant relationship (at the .05 level of confidence) for the Eighty-fifth Congress. In 1939, practically all internationalists were Democrats and practically all isolationists were Republicans.

The regional voting patterns outlined by Rieselbach are similar to those identified by previous research. The most internationalist of the regional groups in the Eighty-third and Eighty-fifth Congresses were East and Pacific Coast legislators (p. 583). Midwestern isolationism did not characterize members from both parties but was confined to Republican representatives. During this twenty-year period southern Democrats tended to give progressively less support to international programs although southern Republicans did not become less internationalist. As the relationship between party and foreign aid scale positions declined, demographic characteristics as well as region assumed added importance. Ruralism became more closely associated with an isolationist position, whereas high ethnicity, high socio-economic status, high levels of education, and urbanism became associated with an internationalist position. Rieselbach concluded that the importance of constituency characteristics is inversely related to party cohesion as a determinant of Congressional votes. Thus a curious and unclear relationship was found: during certain periods members of the same party voted together; at other times members of like constituencies and regions voted together.

Rieselbach (1966a) later attacked the problem of unidimensionality of foreign affairs voting in the House. He found that during the Eighty-eighth Congress votes on funds for the Arms Control and Disarmament Agency and the RS-70 manned bomber would not scale with votes for foreign aid authorizations and appropriations. His cross-tabulations indicated that Democrats, easterners, westerners, high socioeconomic districts, urban constituencies, and districts high in foreign stock tended to support the internationalist-multilateralist position. Republicans, southerners, low socioeconomic districts, low urban constituencies, and districts low in foreign stock were lower in their support for internationalist-multilateralist programs. These findings substantiate other studies of earlier Congresses (Rieselbach, 1964; Grassmuck, 1951; Westerfield, 1955).

From 1945–1962, the relationship between the urbanism of a district and foreign affairs voting was substantial. Havens (1964) used partial correlations to control for the effects of party, region, and the incidence of manufacturing and agriculture to assess the importance of metropolitan areas on foreign policy and national security votes. Although party affiliation was more important than any other single factor, urbanization was more important than region on foreign aid and trade issues. His findings support Rieselbach's (1966) concerning the decline of party conflict concerning foreign affairs votes:

> The division of foreign aid attitudes along urban-rural lines in Congress became steadily more important through the 1950's, as the impact of party discipline declined and sectional patterns disappeared from most roll calls in this field (p. 762–763).

Rieselbach (1964, p. 584) convincingly demonstrated that congressmen from urban districts, since the Eightieth Congress, have been more internationalist than their colleagues from rural areas. Havens

(p. 766) further asserts that urbanization is more important than the economic attributes of constituencies on foreign affairs votes.

The studies cited in Chapter 2 relating party competition to roll-call behavior did not include foreign affairs votes as dependent variables. Havens (1964) and Rieselbach (1966) both study this question. Rieselbach (pp. 88–93) points out that the relationship between these variables has reversed itself from the Seventy-sixth to the Eighty-fifth Congress. In the Eighty-third and Eighty-fifth Congresses there was a tendency for representatives from competitive districts to be more internationalist than isolationist. Havens, however, found "only a slight and statistically insignificant tendency for congressmen from marginal districts to support the president (if from their own party) more often than [did] their politically secure colleagues" (p. 769). Although Rieselbach offers an interesting explanation for his findings —that, as public opinion has become more favorable to foreign aid, representatives from marginal districts have reflected this change in their voting—the strength of this relationship is very weak. This is true even for Rieselbach's data which reports only a correlation of —.24 between electoral margin and foreign aid voting (p. 90).

As the research findings have shown, the effect of constituency on foreign affairs votes is not stable over a length of time (Rieselbach, 1964) or across regions (Westerfield, 1955). In addition to the dynamic relationship between demographic characteristics of constituency and foreign affairs voting, Miller and Stokes (1963) have demonstrated that foreign affairs votes tend to be unrelated to the foreign affairs attitudes of constituents.

Southern congressional voting on foreign affairs is an instance in which the relationship between region and roll-call behavior has changed over time. Throughout the thirties and forties, southerners tended to be internationalists (Lerche, 1964, p. 23; Grassmuck, 1951, p. 102). During the fifties, they started casting more isolationist votes (Rieselbach, 1964, p. 582), leading political scientists to inquire into the correlates of this change. Jewell (1959) concluded that:

> Southern senators were inclined to vote for measures even when presented by a Republican administration, that were closely identified with the Democratic administration or with a traditional Democratic position (p. 637).

This is related to a proposition Grassmuck (1951, p. 102) suggested: When region is highly identified with party, the region will support issues enhancing the success of the party. According to this view southern democrats supported the internationalist programs of the Democratic administration during the thirties and forties, but, in the fifties, as the foreign affairs proposals of the Republican administration became less and less associated with previous Democratic programs, southern congressmen took a more isolationist position.

Lerche (1964) attempted to interpret the southern drift in terms of demographic constituency characteristics. That he was unable to do so successfully supports the position of MacRae (1958), Westerfield (1955), Rieselbach (1964), and Miller and Stokes (1963) who proposed that no strong and/or consistent relationship exists between constituency and foreign affairs roll calls.

The Grassmuck and Jewell proposition seems to explain foreign affairs votes of southern congressmen from 1930 to 1960, but it does not explain why these congressmen did not revert to an internationalist position under the Democratic presidencies of Kennedy and Johnson during the 1960's. The explanation of this behavior may be found in a modification of the Grassmuck proposition related to the basis and nature of southern loyalty to the Democratic party. It is well-known that southern loyalty to the Democratic party solidified during the Reconstruction era and that southern insurgence on congressional roll calls is related to racial issues (Key, 1949, pp. 350ff. and 370ff.). Although southern congressmen are more loyal to the racial position of the white South than to the Democratic party, insurgence on foreign affairs roll calls might also be expected as the Democratic party became identified as the party of civil rights. Southern alienation within the Democratic party was visible when the "solid South" broke with the Democratic party, for the first time in more than one hundred years, during the 1964 presidential election. Insurgence on foreign affairs roll calls also seems to be a product of regional party conflict. A revised proposition is that when regional attitudes and interests are necessary for electoral victory, and when region and party conflict, congressional behavior will reflect regional rather than party interests. This proposition may suggest a partial explanation of southern roll-call behavior, but it must be noted that fewer clear-cut regularities have related the South to foreign affairs voting than have been found for other regions. This should be kept in mind when the performance of the simulation model across regions is discussed.

SELECTING AND CODING ROLL CALLS

The research literature on foreign affairs voting provides a basis for experimenting with the model on foreign policy roll calls in the same way that the general legislative behavior research provided a basis for the original construction of the computer model. The basic system of coding foreign affairs roll calls and some of the latter experiments were based on the propositions discussed.

The only a priori, theoretical requirement imposed on the selection of votes was that they be concerned with foreign affairs during the Eighty-eighth Congress. The *Congressional Quarterly Almanac* (1963, 1964) listing of foreign affairs roll calls constituted the sample for the present experiments. Each bill was coded solely on the basis of information provided by the *Congressional Quarterly Almanac*. Needless to say this did not include the actual votes of any representative. For the first simulation run a basic coding system was developed that included (1) party introducing the measure, (2) committee reporting the proposal, (3) sponsor, (4) minority reporters, (5) party, region, and state of the president, and (6) a notation indicating whether a high score for foreign affairs support would tend to favor or oppose the vote. Region and constituency factors, although related to foreign affairs roll calls in prior studies were not included in the basic coding because of the tentative, indirect nature of their relationship. Experiments with region and constituency characteristics coded as salient to foreign affairs voting are reported in Chapter 8.

Four of the 31 roll calls reported by the *Congressional Quarterly Almanac* as foreign affairs votes were not included in the simulation runs.[1] These included votes on which the president did not take a position, on which the parties did not take a stand, or on issues not related to major foreign affairs issues.

Five of the votes simulated were bipartisan measures which ranged

[1] The roll calls excluded from the study were: (1) a motion ordering the previous question on HR 5517; (2) a motion waiving points of order on HR 11812; (3) a motion to adopt conference report on HR 8864; and (4) a motion for an open rule for debate on HR 539.

TABLE 13. Foreign Policy Roll Calls of the Eighty-eighth Congress Processed by the Model

Roll Call	Description
HR 4374	Authorize the president to proclaim Winston Churchill an honorary citizen of the United States.
HR 5517 (*recommittal*)	Supplemental foreign aid appropriations for fiscal 1963. The recommittal motion was to instruct the House conferees to disagree to the contribution to the International Peace Corps.
HR 3872	A motion by Patman (D, Tex.) instructing House delegates to disagree with proposed Senate "backdoor" financing for the Export-Import Bank of Washington.
HR 5207	A motion to adopt a special rule waiving points of order against ungermane amendments that added to the bill a Philippine war claims rider.
HR 7885 (*recommittal*)	A motion by Adair (R, Ind.) to recommit the foreign aid bill to the Foreign Affairs Committee and make substantial cuts.
HR 7885	A bill to authorize appropriation of $3.5 billion for foreign aid for fiscal 1964.
HR 8864	A bill to authorize the president to limit coffee imports and require certificates of origin from exporting countries in accord with the International Coffee Agreement of 1962.
H Report 863—S 777	A two year authorization of a $20 million appropriation for the Arms Control and Disarmament Agency.
HR 7885	Foreign Assistance Act of 1963 which authorized appropriation of $3.6 billion for 1964.
HR 9499 (*recommittal*)	Jenson (R, Iowa) moved to recommit the Foreign Aid Appropriation Bill and insert an amendment barring the Export-Import Bank from guaranteeing credits to Communist

TABLE 13. *(Continued)*

Roll Call	Description
	nations or their nationals for purchase of U. S. commodities.
HR 9499	The Foreign Aid Appropriations bill for 1964.
HR 9499	A motive to waive the rule for a one day layover from conference report to floor action.
HR 9499 *(recommittal)*	A motion instructing House conferees to disagree to the Senate amendment deleting the House ban on Export-Import credits to Communist countries.
HR 9499	A motion to waive the rule for a one day layover from the second conference report to floor action.
HR 9499	A motion by Passman (D, La.) permitting the president to authorize Export-Import Bank credit to Communist nations if in the national interest after providing Congress with a thirty day notice.
HR 9022 *(recommittal)*	Talcott (R, Cal.) moved to recommit to the Banking and Currency Committee a bill authorizing $312 million to increase the financial resources of the International Development Association.
S 2455 *(recommittal)*	Gross (R. Iowa) moved to recommit a bill authorizing $115 million for Peace Corps operations in fiscal 1965 with instructions to reduce the authorization to $95.9 million.
S 2214 *(recommittal)*	Clawson (R, Cal.) moved to recommit a bill authorizing $312 million for the International Development Agency.
HR 11380 *(recommittal)*	Adair (R, Ind.) moved to recommit the Foreign Assistance Act of 1964 with instructions to reduce the 1965 fiscal authorization.
HR 11380	A bill authorizing $2.041 billion to foreign aid appropriations for fiscal 1965.

TABLE 13. *(Continued)*

Roll Call	Description
HR 11812 *(recommittal)*	Rhodes (R, Ariz.) moved to recommit to the Appropriations Committee the Foreign Aid Bill of 1964 with instructions to reduce economic funds by $247.8 million.
HR 11812	A bill appropriating $3.3 billion for foreign assistance and $422 million for related programs.
HJ Res 1145	A resolution supporting the president's actions in retaliating to attacks against U.S. naval forces of Viet Nam.
H Res 836	A rule providing for debate on S 1451 giving jurisdiction to U.S. Court of Claims in the General Dyestuff Corp. Case.
S 1627	A bill to enable the U.S. to pay its share for the International Commission for Supervision and Control in Laos.
H Con Res 343	A resolution expressing concern for getting nations in arrears in their UN payments to pay their assessments.
S 2701	A bill to authorize a five member commission to study the feasibility for a new interoceanic canal in Central America.

from a resolution granting honorary citizenship to Winston Churchill to the authorization of a five-member commission to study the feasibility of a proposed new interoceanic canal (Table 13). These five measures were coded (Table 14) as bipartisan votes and so that a high foreign affairs support score would favor a yes vote. Other codings in these two sample cases included Francis Walter (D, Pa.) as sponsor of the Churchill resolution, with the House Committee on Merchant Marine and Fisheries reporting out the interocean canal study, and with H. R. Gross (R, Iowa) opposed to it.

The Democratic administration introduced and supported 13 of the simulated roll calls. These votes included five decisions on foreign aid authorization and appropriation, five votes on international treaty and foreign commitments, two procedural votes, and an authorization of funds for the Arms Control and Disarmament Agency.[2] Under the basic coding system, these bills were coded as Democratic bills, so that a high foreign affairs support score, that is "memory" score, would favor a yes vote, and the relevant committees, sponsors, and minority reporters were included along with the president in the communication system.

A third group of roll calls consisted of nine Republican sponsored recommittal motions. Four of these motions were aimed at sending the foreign aid bill back to committee with instructions to reduce funds tagged for authorization or appropriation. The other five recommittal efforts were aimed at imposing various other constraints on administration programs. They were coded as Republican roll calls, a low foreign affairs support score was coded to favor a yes vote, and the sponsor of the motion or the Republican leadership was coded in support of the vote. The president was also included in the communication system to confront representatives since his program was the target of these recommittal motions.

PERFORMANCE OF THE MODEL ON THE BASIC ROLL-CALL CODING SYSTEM

As in assessing the model's performance on domestic roll calls, a check was made regarding the amount of stochastic variation in the communication process for foreign affairs roll calls. To determine the range of this variation, two votes were processed repeatedly by the simulation. One of the roll calls, HR 8864, had a relatively small number of congressional votes determined as it entered the communication stage, and the other, HR 12, had a relatively large number determined. By coding just memory on HR 8864, the votes of 290 congressmen were undecided upon entering the communication stage. The percent agreement between the simulated and the actual votes varied from: 85, 87, 86, 86, 87, 85, 86, 86, 86, 85, and 86. By following the basic roll-call coding model for HR 12, the votes of 151 congressmen remained to be determined during the communication stage. The percent agreement between the votes varied from: 84, 84, 84, 84, 84, 84, 85, 84, 84 and 84. In neither case, with either a high or low number of votes determined during the individual stage, was there a large variation in performance.

[2] This bill, as noted by Rieselbach (1966a), did not scale with the other bills.

TABLE 14. The Coding of Foreign Affairs Roll Calls

| | Constituency (Percentage) | | | | | | | | | | | | | | President | | | | |
Roll Call	Party	State	Region	Urban	Rural Non-Farm	Rural Farm	Negro	Foreign stock	Own Occ H'sing	White Collar	Plurality	Competitiveness	Committees	Minority Repts.	Sponsorship	Party	State	Region	Foreign Affairs Support Score
HR 4374	3												12		409	1	21	1	1
HR 5517*	2														231	1	21	1	2
HR 3872	3														297	1	21	1	2
HR 5207	1												02		004	1	21	1	1
HR 7885*	2												07		261	1	21	1	2
HR 7885	1													007, 085[a]	135	1	21	1	2
HR 8864	1												20	155, 365	195	1	21	1	1
H Rpt 863—S 777	1												07		296	1	21	1	1
HR 7885	1												07			1	43	2	1
HR 9499*	2															1	43	2	2
HR 9499	1												02			1	43	2	1
HR 9499	1														322	1	43	2	1
HR 9499*	2														296	1	43	2	2
HR 9499	1													322, 125	385	1	43	2	1
HR 9499	1													321		1	43	2	1
HR 9022*	2														155	1	43	2	2
S 2455*	2														104	1	43	2	2
S 2214*	2															1	43	2	2

HR 11380*	2			04	1	43	2	2
HR 11380	1	07	004, 155		1	43	2	1
			033, 096					
HR 11812*	2			32	2	43	2	2
HR 11812	1	02			1	43	2	1
HJ Res 1145	3				1	43	2	1
H Res 836	3				1	43	2	1
S 1627	1				1	43	2	1
H Con Res 343	3				1	43	2	1
S 2701	1	13	155		1	43	2	1

* Signifies recommittal motions.

ᵃ Three digit numbers are used to identify individual congressmen.

Coding Index

PARTY
  Democrat 1
  Republican 2
  Bipartisan 3

REGION
  East 1
  South 2

STATE
  Massachusetts 21
  Texas 43

COMMITTEES
  Appropriations 02
  Foreign Affairs 07
  Judiciary 12
  Merchant Marine and Fisheries 13

FOREIGN AFFAIRS SUPPORT SCORE
  "Internationalist" 1
  "Isolationist" 2

On the basis of the basic roll-call coding system (Table 15) the Pearson product-moment coefficient of correlation between the simulated and actual yeas was .91, for the nays, .91, and for the yea-nay split, .89.[3] The basic coding produced an average agreement of 84 percent between the simulated and the actual votes.

The model produced 85 percent agreement for Democrats and 82 percent for Republicans. A partial explanation of this difference is suggested by a feature of the model and by the research literature. Legislative research has abundantly demonstrated that when the majority party controls the executive it tends to be cohesive in support of the administration whereas the minority tends to be more fluid and divided (Turner, 1951, p. 42; Westerfield, 1955, p. 46; Grassmuck, 1951, p. 140; Matthews, 1960, p. 143; Truman, 1959, p. 281). Since the Republicans did not control the White House during the Eighty-eighth Congress, its voting structure should have been more fluid and less predictable than the majority party. When this notion is combined with the design feature of the model that included the president in interactions with House members, especially House Democrats, greater cohesion and accuracy would be expected for the majority party.

The differential levels of agreement between high and low seniority congressmen is considerably larger than the difference between the parties. The agreement between the simulated and the actual votes for low seniority members was 87 percent; the agreement for high seniority members was 78 percent. In considering these differences it should be noted that 71 of the low seniority congressmen did not have a foreign affairs support score at the beginning of each simulation run because they were in their freshman term. Truman (1959, p. 212) demonstrated the existence of an inverse relationship between seniority and support of the floor leader. Because the simulation model has a strong tendency to assign the position of the party to its elected leadership, we would expect party regulars in both the simulation and the House to be overrepresented among low seniority members. What apparently happens in the simulation is that both low and high seniority members are assigned approximately the same rate of party regularity, variables other than party reduce the party loyalty of high seniority members more in the House than in the simulation model.

---

[3] Because these correlation coefficients are markedly similar, only the yea-nay correlation will be reported in the future.

Garceau and Silverman (1954) and Silverman (1954) give additional support to this explanation, pointing out that higher party regularity should be expected from neophyte legislators. A direct and positive relationship was found between the complexity of political conflict perceived by legislators and length of service. Freshmen and low seniority members tended to see political conflict almost entirely along party lines; high seniority congressmen perceived, in addition,

TABLE 15. The "Basic Coding" Model Simulation

Roll Call		Actual Voting	Percent Correct	Simulated Voting
HR 4374		378—21	94.7	399—0
HR 5517	(recommittal)	207—190	89.2	133—164
HR 3872		379—11	97.2	390—0
HR 5207		234—166	80.5	263—137
HR 7885	(recommittal)	222—188	79.5	149—261
HR 7885		224—186	74.9	262—148
HR 8864		181—145	81.6	211—145
H Report 863—S 777		251—134	72.9	245—140
HR 7885		195—164	75.0	225—134
HR 9499	(recommittal)	218—169	79.6	141—246
HR 9499		250—135	76.4	249—136
HR 9499		182—95	88.4	158—119
HR 9499	(recommittal)	141—136	87.7	110—167
HR 9499		202—105	97.4	196—111
HR 9499		189—158	90.8	218—129
HR 9022	(recommittal)	208—189	76.0	157—240
S 2455	(recommittal)	90—309	81.0	146—249
S 2214	(recommittal)	132—247	73.6	153—226
HR 11380	(recommittal)	193—211	85.6	155—249
HR 11380		230—175	73.6	246—159
HR 11812	(recommittal)	198—208	82.0	153—253
HR 11812		231—174	72.6	253—152
HJ Res 1145		416—0	100.0	416—0
H Res 836	(procedural)	375—3	99.2	318—0
S 1627		268—89	76.8	204—153
H Con Res 343		352—0	100.0	352—0
S 2701		320—23	90.8	320—23

The average percent correct for these simulated votes was 84.3.
The product-moment correlation between the simulated and actual yeas was .91, for the nays, .91, and for the yea-nay split, .89.

interest group and other types of conflict. Because the model treats party affiliation as a major determinant of legislative voting it would be expected to represent more accurately members who tend to be party regulars, such as low seniority members.

The simulation produced considerable variation across regional groupings. The agreement between the simulated and House votes was 85 percent for easterners, 74 percent for southerners, 89 percent for midwesterners, 88 percent for Mountain congressmen, and 92 percent for West Coast representatives. Some of the error for southern congressmen is probably due to the Republican-southern Democratic conservative coalition; in no case was this coalition coded as salient to a roll call. Failure to code the conservative coalition on votes would depress performance for southern Democrats but should not depreciate the prediction of Republican votes.

A second source of error for southern congressmen is suggested in a study by Froman and Ripley (1965, p. 40). During the Eighty-eighth Congress, the Democratic House whip office polled Democratic congressmen on 10 important roll calls to determine their: (1) presence or absence, and (2) vote intention. Southern Democrats were consistently overrepresented in that group of congressmen, producing the greatest amount of error in the poll. This second source of error, then, is that southern Democrats tend to be less loyal to the party than other Democratic legislators. Proposition 48 also suggested lower performance for southerners than for other regional groupings; they have tended to be inconsistent in their foreign affairs votes. Finally, the proposition mentioned in the discussion of southern foreign affairs roll-call research, that the intensity of regional-party conflict over civil rights disrupted party loyalty in other issue areas, suggests that southern congressmen will be underrepresented among party regulars in foreign affairs voting in the 1960's, thus depressing the model's performance. The research literature on region and roll-call behavior does not offer an explanation for the variation of 8 percent among legislators from outside the South. It should be noted that the variation among non-South regions is 8 percent, when the South is included the variation jumps to 18 percent.

The representativeness of simulation output varies for different types of roll calls. Bipartisan roll calls were replicated with greater accuracy than were either Democrat or Republican sponsored votes. Bipartisan accuracy was 98 percent, for Democratic roll calls it was 82 percent, and for Republican votes it was 86 percent. The model works less well for bills of high conflict. Employing a criteria in which at least 20 percent of those voting opposed the majority (Turner, 1951), the basic coding of the foreign affairs vote produced 81 percent agreement between the simulated and the actual votes.

Summary

On an initial coding system developed to evaluate the simulation model, the simulation postdicted an average of more than 84 percent of the votes cast on 27 roll calls and the simulated yea-nay splits correlated .89 with the actual splits. As was expected, on the basis of legislative research and theory, the model performed better (1) for the majority than for the minority party, (2) for low seniority than for high seniority congressmen, (3) for non-southern than for southern representatives. The model, as expected, apparently simulates the behavior of party regulars more accurately than the behavior of insurgents. In order to investigate alternative formulations of the simulation model, we next employed a strategy that parallels that reported in Chapter 6, sensitivity testing.

The Validity of
the Simulation Model:
Alternative Formulations on
Foreign Affairs Votes

In Chapter 1 it was argued that the validity of the simulation is a question of how well the model represents the referent system. The most straightforward approach in attempting to validate a simulation is to compare its operations with *known* characteristics of its referent. Also, simulation validity may be partly considered a discovery process (Kress, 1966). When a simulation based on extant theory is constructed, we do not know exactly how it will operate because we do not know exactly how the reference system operates. If we knew this, there would be little scientific interest in simulating it.

As has been suggested, simulation models may be manipulated in ways that are usually impossible in "real-world laboratories." Results of simulation experiments may suggest relationships about the phenomena under investigation that have gone unnoticed. If it is possible to return to the referent and substantiate discoveries made during a simulation run, further validation of the model will have occurred by discovering this new information. For example, legislative behavior research has noted that interpersonal interactions are an important aspect of legislative behavior (Propositions 25–29). By manipulating the model it may be possible to help assess the role of intra-legislative communication in roll-call voting. One step toward validating the model would be taken if propositions derived from simulation outcomes are found to hold for the House. To facilitate such an investigation the propositions suggested by simulation experiments will be formally stated throughout the chapter. In the following experiments the contribution of several variables will be alternately examined in an effort to clarify existing theory.

THE EFFECT OF REGION AND CONSTITUENCY

The basic coding system for foreign affairs votes did not treat any region or constituency variables as salient. Research reviewed in Chapter 7, however, notes several relationships that have been found between region, constituency type, and foreign affairs votes. A question raised by these findings is whether region and constituency produce separate and distinct influences on foreign affairs votes, apart from memory, for each individual. Across all 27 roll calls, eastern and Pacific congressmen were coded as pro-internationalist, and southern congressmen as anti-internationalist. The average agreement between the simulated votes and the actual votes dropped from 84.3 percent for the basic coding system to 83.7 percent where region was added.

In relating constituency characteristics to foreign affairs votes, high urban, high socioeconomic, and high foreign stock districts were coded to favor a pro-administration, pro-internationalist position. High rural farm districts were coded as anti-internationalist. After constituency as well as region were added to the basic coding for each roll call, the average percent agreement dropped to 83. The second measurement employed, the correlation of the yea-nay split between the simulated and the actual votes, produced a correlation of .89 for the basic coding system, .86 when region was added, and .83 when constituency and region were added to the basic code. Across this sample of roll calls, therefore, adding region and constituency to the basic coding system depressed the performance of the model at both the micro and macro levels.

For 7 of the 27 votes adding regions and constituency improved the performance of the simulation. This subset of votes, underlined in Table 16, included all final roll calls on foreign aid authorization and appropriation, support for the Arms Control and the Disarmament Agency, and International Development Agency. Only one of these seven measures was a recommittal motion. The basic coding for these seven major issues produced simulate-referent agreement of 74 percent, by adding region and constituency the percent of agreement was raised to 80.

The characteristics that set this group of roll calls apart are two-fold: (1) these votes, all on important substantive issues, were closely related to the administration's foreign policy proposals, and (2) these roll calls had more visibility than other administration proposals and other Republican recommittal motions. Even the recommittal vote on S 2214 had been the subject of prolonged debate and newspaper coverage by the time of the final roll call (*Congressional Quarterly Almanac*, 1963, p. 634). The effect of visibility on roll-call behavior and leadership effectiveness had been noted by Froman and Ripley (1965, p. 59) as a case in which constituency and regional attitudes or communications become salient to the vote reducing party cohesiveness. Whereas, on many roll calls, congressmen may ignore audiences from "back home" either because there is no clear opinion or because local groups are not aware of the vote, these seven issues were both important and visible.

By adding region and constituency to the other 20 roll calls the percent agreement dropped from 84 to 79. In view of these results we may conclude:

1) Coding region and constituency characteristics as salient to all foreign affairs roll calls decreased the representativeness of the model.

2) On a subset of seven visible, substantive roll calls regional and constituency attributes were salient to foreign affairs votes and by coding bills on these dimensions, the representativeness of the model was increased.

3) On a subset of 20 roll calls that included several recommittal and bipartisan votes, including region and constituency as salient noticeably decreased the representativeness of the model.

TABLE 16. The Addition of Region and Constituency to the "Basic Coding" Model.

Roll Call		Actual Votes	Percent[a] Correct	Basic Model Plus Region Votes
HR 4374		378—21	94.7	[b]390—0
HR 5517	(recommittal)	207—190	74.1	105—292
HR 3872		379—11	97.2	390—0
HR 5207		234—166	77.5	293—107
HR 7885	(recommittal)	222—188	73.2	119—291
HR 7885		224—186	76.1[d]	288—119
HR 8864		181—145	77.6	227—99
H Report 863—S777		251—134	78.4	277—108
HR 7885		195—164	76.4	252—107
HR 9499	(recommittal)	218—169	78.8	144—243
HR 9499		250—135	74.5	271—174
HR 9499		182—95	91.3	168—109
HR 9499	(recommittal)	141—136	83.0	94—183
HR 9499		202—105	97.4	196—111
HR 9499		189—158	86.2	237—110
HR 9022	(recommittal)	208—189	74.7	132—265
S 2455		90—309	80.0	140—259
S 2214	(recommittal)	132—247	78.9	154—225
HR 11380	(recommittal)	193—211	82.2	137—267
HR 11380		230—175	79.0	273—132
HR 11812	(recommittal)	198—208	81.5	135—271
HR 11812		231—174	77.0	272—133
RJ Res 1145		416—0	100.0	416—0
H Res 836		375—3	99.2	378—0
S 1627		268—89	81.8	227—130
H Con Res 343		352—0	100.0	352—0
S 2701		320—23	91.6	329—14

[a] The average percent correct when region was added to the basic coding model was 83.7, when constituency and region were added the average percent correct was 82.7.

[b] The correlation between the actual yeas and the simulated yeas produced by the basic coding model plus region was .86, for the nays it was .86 and the correlation of the yea-nay split was .86.

TABLE 16. (*Continued*)

Roll Call		Percent Correct	Basic Model Plus Region and Constituency
HR 4374		94.7	c390—0
HR 5517	(recommittal)	70.5	94—303
HR 3872		97.2	390—0
HR 5207		70.2	206—194
HR 7885	(recommittal)	71.2	105—305
HR 7885		74.1	306—104
HR 8864		73.0	238—88
H Report 863—S 777		78.9	288—97
HR 7885		75.8	260—99
HR 9499	(recommittal)	73.4	125—262
HR 9499		77.7	283—102
HR 9499		91.0	169—108
HR 9499	(recommittal)	81.2	92—185
HR 9499		97.4	196—111
HR 9499		80.7	248—99
HR 9022	(recommittal)	75.0	128—269
S 2455		74.5	140—259
S 2214	(recommittal)	82.8	124—256
HR 11380	(recommittal)	82.4	127—277
HR 11380		81.0	277—128
HR 11812	(recommittal)	82.8	133—273
HR 11812		83.7	274—131
RJ Res 1145		100.0	416—0
H Res 836		99.2	378—0
S 1627		79.6	226—131
H Con Res 343		100.0	252—0
S 2701		90.8	320—23

c The correlation between the actual yeas and the simulated yeas when constituency factors were added to the coding was .83, for the nays it was .84, and for the yea-nay split it was .83.

d The roll calls whose representativeness was increased by including region and/or constituency in the coding are underlined.

TABLE 17. The "Just Party" Model and the "Without Party" Model
Simulations

Roll Call		Actual Votes	Percent Correct[a]	"Just Party" Votes
HR 4374		378—21	94.7[d]	[b]398—0
HR 5517	(recommittal)	207—190	89.2	164—233
HR 3872		379—11	97.2	390—0
HR 5207		234—166	79.5	233—167
HR 7885	(recommittal)	222—188	79.5	171—239
HR 7885		224—186	71.0	239—171
HR 8864		181—145	85.6	191—135
H Report 863—S 777		251—134	69.3	228—156
HR 7885		195—164	71.1	206—154
HR 9499	(recommittal)	208—169	80.9	158—229
HR 9499		250—135	65.5	230—155
HR 9499		182—95	88.1	157—120
HR 9499	(recommittal)	141—136	89.2	117—160
HR 9499		202—105	97.4	196—111
HR 9499		189—158	91.9	213—134
HR 9022	(recommittal	208—189	75.3	165—231
S 2455	(recommittal)	90—309	71.7	163—237
S 2214	(recommittal)	132—247	71.5	217—162
HR 11380	(recommittal)	193—211	83.2	169—235
HR 11380		230—175	70.9	235—170
HR 11812	(recommittal)	198—208	80.0	165—241
HR 11812		231—174	69.9	240—165
HJ Res 1145		416—0	100.0	416—0
H Res 836		375—3	99.2	378—0
S 1627		268—89	75.9	201—156
H Con Res 343		352—0	100.0	352—0
S 2701		320—23	93.4	343—0

[a]The average percent correct with the just party model was 83.0, the without
party model was correct an average of 72.8 percent.

[b]The correlation between the actual yeas and the simulated yeas for the just
party model was .91, for the nays the correlation was .91, and for the yea-nay
split it was .91.

TABLE 17. *(Continued)*

Roll Call		Percent Correct	"Without Party" Votes
HR 4374		83.2	[c]338—60
HR 5517	(recommittal)	61.2	54—343
HR 3872		00.0	0—18
HR 5207		67.8	350—50
HR 7885	(recommittal)	61.2	62—344
HR 7885		77.6	290—120
HR 8864		68.1	278—48
H Report 863—S 777		80.2	281—102
HR 7885		75.8	257—103
HR 9499	(recommittal)	60.7	66—318
HR 9499		81.8	287—97
HR 9499		85.9	210—66
HR 9499	(recommittal)	75.5	73—203
HR 9499		86.0	233—73
HR 9499		75.5	233—73
HR 9022	(recommittal)	71.2	108—283
S 2455	(recommittal)	81.5	106—294
S 2214	(recommittal)	80.2	109—269
HR 11380	(recommittal)	79.2	111—290
HR 11380		81.5	288—117
HR 11812	(recommittal)	79.1	115—289
HR 11812		82.2	299—117
HJ Res 1145		70.6	294—122
H Res 836		70.9	269—109
S 1627		82.4	244—112
H Con Res 343		75.6	267—85
S 2701		81.2	264—81

[c] The correlation between the actual yeas and the simulated yeas for the without party model was .34, for the nays the correlation was .64 and for the yea-nay split the correlation was .50.

[d] The roll calls whose performance became more representative in the just party and the without party models are underlined.

THE EFFECT OF PARTY

Turner (1951 and 1951a) demonstrated that party affiliation accounts for more congressional voting variance than any other single variable. A formulation of the simulation model suggested by this finding is a just party model to provide voting cues to congressmen and a without party model. Just party coding reduced the accuracy of the postdiction from 84 percent for the basic coding to 83 percent. Although the average percent correct dropped 1, the yea-nay split correlation rose slightly from .89 for the initial coding to .91 for just party. Party, alone, slightly but noticeably increased simulation errors across individual legislators, but overall it produced a covariation at the aggregate level at least as good as the original coding. The expectation, based on legislative research, that party is a good predictor of roll-call behavior, was upheld.

Party exerted a differential impact across these votes as was the case with the region-constituency experiment. On 13 of these 27 foreign affairs issues Table 17 shows that just party coding resulted in postdiction accuracy equal to or greater than performance on the basic code. These 13 roll calls included all five bipartisan votes. Most of the remaining eight issues were Republican recommittal motions introduced with the goal of embarrassing the administration or significantly modifying its proposals. The basic yea-nay correlation across these 13 issues was .95. When just party was coded for each roll call, the coefficient of correlation rose to .99.

Just party coding did not only increase the macro performance of the model, but also upgraded micro accuracy of these votes. The basic code resulted in 91 percent postdiction accuracy, and a slight increase to 92 percent resulted when just party was coded. Of these 13 votes, the just party and the basic code performed identically on eight of the votes. On the remaining five votes, the basic code produced 86 percent agreement and the just party code slightly raised this to 88 percent.

Because coding rules are as much a part of our theoretical model as the computer program itself, parsimony as a desideratum of social science theory should also apply here. In this instance, if a coding model that includes just party performs as well as or superior to a more complex coding system it would seem that these additional variables are either superfluous or actually detract from the representativeness of the simulation.

That some votes seem more closely related to party as an organization, whereas others are related to a more complex set of variables is not unexpected in view of previous research. MacRae (1954), building upon Turner's (1951) earlier findings, demonstrated that identifiable dimensions existed for loyalty to the party both as an organization and as an ideology (Proposition 2). The current 13 votes on which party predicts as well as or more accurately than any feasible theoretical alternative, seems to exemplify loyalty to the party as an organization. If these roll calls had commanded loyalty of an ideological nature, a coding system that emphasized memory—the foreign affairs support score of each representative—would have performed well also. This alternative formulation is not supported by the data. The product-moment coefficient of correlation between the yea-nay splits for a just memory model and the actual votes was only .25 compared to .99 for the just party model. The micro performance of the model dropped to 67 percent correct on the average individual postdictions when just memory was run on these 13 party votes. These 13 roll calls, then, seemed to call forth loyalty to the party as an organization.

The performance of the model was noticeably lowered when a without party model for coding roll calls was processed. The yea-nay split correlation coefficient when the party sponsoring the measure was not included on the coding was .50; the level of agreement between the simulation votes and the actual votes averaged only 73 percent. As with the previous experiments, the performance of the model was increased on a subset of roll calls. The without party model was more representative for nine votes, and these included the seven for which region and constituency proved to be salient. On these substantive votes the correlation of the splits was .82 for the basic coding that included region and constituency factors; when the same coding was retained with the exception of deleting party the correlation of the simulated and actual splits rose to .89. The average percent agreement across these nine votes that included party was 79; the without party model predicted individual votes with an average of 80 percent.

Party may influence roll-call votes in the without party model if two elements are combined: (1) if the parties are distinguished by different distributions of foreign affairs support scores, regions, and constituencies; (2) if the parties are represented in the model by distinct communication nets. In the present experiment, party labels were apparently less important in determining legislative votes than were the different ideological distributions within each party as activated by the communication stage.

Because exclusion of party sponsor on a vote increases the model's representativeness of substantive foreign affairs votes, a proposition is suggested that the party affiliation of the president makes less difference on foreign affairs roll calls than memory and salient regional and constituency audiences. This was in fact the case from 1952 to 1960 when a Republican president found a higher percentage of Democrats supporting his foreign affairs proposals than Republicans.

We may conclude, on the basis of alternative models of coding foreign affairs roll calls in which the independent variable was party sponsorship that:

4) The just party model of coding foreign affairs roll calls produced a slightly less representative performance of the model than did the basic coding scheme.

5) The just party model of coding foreign affairs votes resulted in performance on a subset of 13 roll calls that was equal or superior to the postdiction of the basic coding model.

6) The without party model of coding foreign affairs roll calls produced a more representative output on a subset of nine votes that included the seven measures on which region and constituency proved to be salient, when compared to the basic coding model.

7) The basic coding model performed better than either the just party or the without party model on five roll calls.

8) There are three kinds of foreign affairs roll calls that command: (1) loyalty to party as an organization, as exemplified by those measures on which party label produces the highest comparative level of representativeness, (2) loyalty to party as an ideology, as represented by those votes on which the without party model resulted in comparatively superior performance, and (3) loyalty to both party organization and ideology, which is represented by the five bills on which the basic coding model worked better comparatively.

THE EFFECT OF MEMORY

To establish the contribution of memory to the foreign affairs support scores, the bills were processed with just memory and without memory (Table 18). The just memory model produced a coefficient of correlation between the simulated yea-nay split and the actual split across the sample of 27 votes of .33; the without memory model produced a correlation coefficient of the splits of .90. The average level of postdiction accuracy was 73 percent with just memory and 84 percent with the without memory model.

One would expect the just memory model to correlate relatively higher with the without party model and with the substantive roll calls. The correlation between the just memory and the without party models is .79, and is .86 between just memory and the substantive yea-nay splits. It should be remembered, however, that the without party model correlated .89 with the actual splits on the substantive roll calls. The higher correlation would seem to be due to the regional and constituency audiences that were coded as salient in the without party model.

One would also expect the without memory model to correlate relatively higher with the just party model and the subset of party and procedural votes. The without memory model correlates .92 with the just party model, and .98 with the party and procedural roll calls.

The correlation between the just party and the just memory splits is a relatively low, .25. This is in contrast to the finding that the just party and the just memory splits correlate .62 for domestic issues on the expanding role of the federal government. This difference between the apparent determinants of foreign and domestic roll-call issues is expected because the differences between the parties is clearest and most consistent on social class issues, appropriation measures, and on votes to embarrass the administration (Turner, 1951; Keefe, 1952). Because the regularity of party members is lower on foreign affairs, intra-party variance will be higher than on domestic issues producing a lower correlation between the just party and the just memory models.

As a result of the experiments with memory we may conclude that:

9) The just memory model was quite non-representative of actual roll-call voting on this sample of foreign affairs issues.

TABLE 18. The "Just Memory" Model and the "Without Memory" Model
Simulations

Roll Call		Actual Votes	Percent Correct[a]	"Just Memory" Votes
HR 4374		378—21	81.2	[b]326—72
HR 5517	(recommittal)	207—190	60.2	51—342
HR 3872	(recommittal)	379—11	00.0	0—20
HR 5207		234—166	71.5	326—72
HR 7885	(recommittal)	222—188	65.1	77—333
HR 7885		224—186	72.7	323—84
HR 8864		181—145	70.9	254—68
H Report 863—S 777		251—134	78.6	301—81
HR 7885		195—164	74.4	281—78
HR 9499	(recommittal)	218—169	62.3	72—313
HR 9499		250—135	79.7	288—94
HR 9499		182—95	87.7	189—84
HR 9499	(recommittal)	141—136	80.1	86—188
HR 9499		202—105	87.9	217—90
HR 9499		189—158	83.9	235—108
HR 9022	(recommittal)	208—189	72.0	114—275
S 2455	(recommittal)	90—309	82.0	120—280
S 2214	(recommittal)	132—247	77.8	110—267
HR 11380	(recommittal)	193—211	80.4	119—279
HR 11380		230—175	80.7	269—133
HR 11812	(recommittal)	198—208	80.5	125—278
HR 11812		231—174	80.0	277—125
HJ Res 1145		416—0	67.7	283—130
H Res 836		375—3	68.3	259—115
S 1627		268—89	83.8	250—102
H Con Res 343		352—0	72.5	256—97
S 2701		320—23	77.2	254—89

[a] The average percent correct for the just memory model was 72.6; it was 83.9
for the without memory model.

[b] The correlation between the actual and simulated yeas for the just memory
model was .37, for the nays the correlation was .43, and for the yea-nay split it
was .43.

TABLE 18. *(Continued)*

Roll Call	Percent Correct	"Without Memory" Votes
HR 4374	[c]94.7[d]	389—0
HR 5517 (recommittal)	89.2	164—233
HR 3872 (recommittal)	97.2	390—0
HR 5207	78.8	235—165
HR 7885 (recommittal)	79.5	171—239
HR 7885	71.7	287—121
HR 8864	85.9	192—134
H Report 863—S 777	73.7	267—113
HR 7885	73.3	256—102
HR 9499 (recommittal)	80.9	158—229
HR 9499	74.0	282—101
HR 9499	88.4	158—119
HR 9499 (recommittal)	89.2	117—160
HR 9499	97.4	196—111
HR 9499	90.8	217—128
HR 9022 (recommittal)	75.3	165—231
S 2455 (recommittal)	71.7	163—237
S 2214 (recommittal)	74.1	117—259
HR 11380 (recommittal)	83.2	169—235
HR 11380	72.8	285—118
HR 11812 (recommittal)	80.3	166—240
HR 11812	76.0	282—119
HJ Res 1145	100.0	416—0
H Res 836	99.2	378—0
S 1627	75.9	201—156
H Con Res 343	100.0	352—0
S 2701	93.4	343—0

[c] The correlation between the actual and simulated yeas for the without memory model was .89, for the nays the correlation was .89, and for the yea-nay split it was .90.

[d] The roll calls whose performance became more representative in the just memory and the without memory models are underlined.

10)   The just memory model and the just party model were not substitutes on foreign affairs roll calls as they were for domestic issues.

11)   The just memory model was significantly related to the without party model and to actual votes on substantive roll calls.

12)   The without memory model was significantly related to the just party model and to actual party and procedural voting.

A Revised Coding System Based on the Experiments

It has become evident, as the various experiments have been performed, that the representativeness of the model could be improved by slightly altering the basic coding model. These experiments have enabled us to categorize inductively the bills as (a) party or procedural, (b) substantive, or (c) a party and substantive combination. We have found that the without party model on substantive issues and the just party model on party and procedural issues increases the postdictive accuracy of the simulation. Of the 27 roll calls processed, 13 were party or procedural, nine were substantive, and the remaining five represented a combination of party and substantive interests.

Whereas the basic coding system produced an average of 84 percent agreement between the simulated and the referent system, the revised coding system raised this postdiction accuracy slightly to 86 percent. Whereas the correlation coefficient of the yea-nay splits between the basic coding system and the actual splits was .89, this correlation was .98 for the revised system.

On the basis of experiments the basic coding model was revised, leading to these conclusions:

13)   A revised coding model increased the representativeness of the model on foreign affairs roll calls.

14)   The revised coding model recognizes three types of roll calls: (a) party or procedural, (b) substantive, and (c) party and substantive.

15)   On the basis of the experiments, substantive and party votes are distinct and non-related.

THE EFFECT OF THE COMMUNICATION STAGE

What role does the communication stage play in the computer representation? This was investigated by removing this stage and studying any change in representativeness that developed (Table 19).

TABLE 19. The "Revised Coding" Model With and Without Communication

Roll Call		Actual Votes	Percent Correct[a]	With Communication Votes
HR 4374		378—21	94.7	[b]399—0
HR 5517	(recommittal)	207—190	89.2	164—233
HR 3872		379—11	97.2	390—0
HR 5207		234—166	80.7	252—248
HR 7885	(recommittal)	222—188	79.5	171—239
HR 7885		224—186	75.6	248—162
HR 8864		181—145	85.9	193—133
H Report 863—S 777		251—134	81.5	253—132
HR 7885		195—164	77.5	212—148
HR 9499	(recommittal)	218—169	80.9	158—229
HR 9499		250—135	79.0	221—163
HR 9499		182—95	90.6	169—106
HR 9499	(recommittal)	141—136	89.2	117—160
HR 9499		189—158	91.9	213—134
HR 9022	(recommittal)	208—189	75.3	162—233
S 2455	(recommittal)	90—309	82.0	63—336
S 2214	(recommittal)	132—247	82.8	124—256
HR 11380	(recommittal)	193—211	83.4	167—236
HR 11380		230—175	81.5	288—117
HR 11812	(recommittal)	198—208	80.5	167—239
HR 11812		231—174	81.2	220—184
HJ Res 1145		416—0	100.0	416—0
H Res 836		375—3	99.2	378—0
S 1627		268—89	83.8	294—62
H Con Res 343		352—0	100.0	352—0
S 2701		320—23	93.4	346—0

[a] The average percent correct for the revised coding model with communication was 86.1, without communication stage it was 83.4.

[b] The correlation between the actual and simulated yeas for the revised coding model was .97, for the nays it was .97, and it was .98 for the yea-nay splits.

TABLE 19. (Continued)

Roll Call		Percent Correct	Without Communication Votes
HR 4374		94.7	c399—0
HR 5517	(recommittal)	89.2	164—233
HR 3872		97.2	390—0
HR 5207		74.7	220—136
HR 7885	(recommittal)	79.5	171—239
HR 7885		69.5	198—159
HR 8864		85.3	194—132
H Report 863—S 777		61.5	164—88
HR 7885		70.8	172—144
HR 9499	(recommittal)	80.9	158—229
HR 9499		70.9	185—156
HR 9499		74.4	127—110
HR 9499	(recommittal)	89.2	117—160
HR 9499		91.9	213—134
HR 9022	(recommittal)	75.8	157—194
S 2455	(recommittal)	53.3	144—135
S 2214	(recommittal)	62.5	128—140
HR 11380	(recommittal)	82.7	158—202
HR 11380		74.8	187—174
HR 11812	(recommittal)	81.0	157—202
HR 11812		76.5	189—176
HJ Res 1145		100.0	416—0
H Res 836		99.2	378—0
S 1627		56.6	124—142
H Con Res 343		100.0	352—0
S 2701		93.4	346—0

c The correlation between the actual and simulated yeas for the revised coding model without the communication stage was .90, for the nays it was .82 and it was .90 for the yea-nay splits.

In executing this experiment, the revised coding model was employed. The coefficient of correlation between the yea-nay split and the model, excluding the communication stage, was .90. The average level of postdiction accuracy without the communication stage was 83 percent.

When the subsets of roll calls identified previously are examined without the communication stage, it is clear that substantive issues were replicated at a much lower level of accuracy. There was only 66 percent average correct postdiction for the without communication stage with the actual substantive votes. This compares with an 80 percent correct prediction for the same coding system with the communication stage. The correlation of the yea-nay splits without communication on the substantive roll calls was .33, and .96 with communication.

Party and procedural votes are unaffected when the communication stage is cut out. In fact, the correlation with or without the communication stage between the simulated and the actual yea-nay splits is .99 for party and procedural roll calls.

The performance of the model is increased by the communication stage. It might be argued that such behavior is an artifact of the model; there may be instances when coding is such that no congressman has his vote determined before entering the communication stage because these individuals do not satisfy the cut-off parameter of a plus or minus two predisposition score. In this respect, on those issues where representativeness declines, it cannot be attributed to "undercoding" the roll calls. For the substantive votes, region and constituency were coded on seven of the nine issues and memory was included on all nine. For the 13 party roll calls, only party sponsor was coded. Apparently the multiple coding of substantive issues placed a number of congressmen under cross-pressures that are normally resolved through communications with other representatives. By removing the means to resolve cross-pressures, agreement between the simulate and the House dropped 14 percent on substantive votes. On party votes the party label itself seems to ensure high agreement with or without interpersonal interaction.

In an attempt to investigate the effect of interpersonal interactions on roll-call behavior we conclude:

16) The representativeness of the model is decreased across the sample of 27 foreign affairs roll calls when the communication stage is excluded.

17) Excluding the communication stage of the model dramatically reduces its performance on substantive foreign affairs votes.

18) Excluding the communication stage of the model does not reduce its performance for party or procedural votes.

19) The communication stage of the model apparently is necessary for the resolution of cross-pressures on foreign affairs issues that is representative of the behavior of congressmen.

20) Little cross-pressures seem to exist on party and procedural roll calls.

Summary

It has been established that the computer model, constructed on the basis of empirical legislative research, simulates roll-call votes that covary at a high level with actual House votes on foreign affairs issues. Simulated votes also agree with actual votes at a relatively high level: 86 percent are correctly postdicted across 27 roll calls. It has been demonstrated that certain regional and constituency characteristics are salient to foreign affairs voting. A just party model has been shown to be more representative on party issues than any alternative model that has been investigated. The without party model is more representative than any of the alternatives studied for substantive issues. Without the communication stage the model is quite non-representative for substantive roll calls; party and procedural votes are not affected. This supports the notion that interpersonal interaction in a legislature may be important in resolving cross-pressures.

A Concluding Note

Traditionally, a variety of approaches have led to the development of empirical political theory. Recently a proliferation of studies based upon the use of quantitative methods have generated sets of propositions relating to legislative behavior and have illuminated, in some detail, many aspects of the roll-call voting process in legislative bodies. Our complex model is a theoretical overview of legislative behavior. As such, it provides a theoretical framework within which the many empirical propositions emerging from legislative behavior research are combined in an attempt to explain this behavior in a scientific manner. However, complex models, unlike the various propositions for which they provide an integrating framework, are not clearly corroborated or falsified by mere exposure to the data they purport to describe and explain. Thus the exposure of our simulation model to domestic and foreign roll-call voting behavior in the Eighty-eighth session of the U. S. House of Representatives is far from conclusive. We cannot, at this point, report on the results of testing individual empirical propositions. Some tentative conclusions are, however, warranted. At the outset we addressed ourselves to the question of the

159

dimensions along which complex theoretical models can be evaluated. Now we may consider our model by bringing together the evaluative criteria with which we began and the subsequent results.

The key dimension along which theories can be evaluated is, of course, the prediction criterion. On this basis our theoretical model has acquitted itself quite well. The predictive ability of the theory is also increased by the clarity of its expression. Using a computer simulation model as an analogue of the theory resulted in an articulation of the theory in clear and operational fashion. Computer instructions prescribed propositions concerning the legislator and his extra-legislative environment, the legislator as an individual political actor, and the legislator in a face-to-face social setting. They also prescribed, in a dynamic manner, the relationships between these attributes of legislators and their roll-call voting behavior. When such prescriptions are expressed in unambiguous operational form, the assessment of their results is all the more compelling.

The overall predictability of the model has important implications for its various components. From the viewpoint of legislative behavior research, the performance of the model lends support to the propositions from the legislative research upon which it is based. While no individual propositions are "tested" in our simulation, the validation of the model, together with the sensitivity testing of its components, addresses itself to the coherence of the propositions which the model combines.

The other criteria for evaluating theories, which we discussed in Chapter 1, are dependent on the prediction criterion we have just assessed. If a theoretical model is an effective predictor, it becomes meaningful to assess its other structural attributes. Thus the ability of the model to simulate legislative voting effectively (i.e., to predict), with relatively few mechanisms grouped into the model's predisposition and communication phases, is suggestive of a positive evaluation in terms of the organizing power criterion. Of course, the model's ability to predict consistently on domestic as well as foreign affairs legislation further enhances this aspect of it.

At a more general level, the model's performance can be assessed in terms of its successful simulation of a large decision-making body. The legislative setting provides convenient validation criteria because of the public character of roll-call votes and their clear status as decision-making variables. While findings on comparative decision-making across legislative and other policy-making institutions are scant, the success of this simulation is encouraging in that application of simulation techniques to the study of social and political processes in a large group has been successful. It is hoped that this type of model can be generalized so that theoretical convergence is obtained and models are developed which explain decision-making processes in a variety of institutional settings.

The results of this simulation should also be considered from a proposition generating as well as a theory building standpoint. Simulations are helpful because of their heuristic value. Both the development of the model and the results of its processing give direction to further research. The construction of the model in the form of precise decisional statements for the computer indicates the areas of research where more testing of empirical propositions is needed. In addition, further research is suggested by some of the results of the computer runs. For example, an unexpected result (at least for the authors) was the differential impact of the communication and influence phase of the model on the prediction of substantive, as opposed to procedural, votes. These kinds of findings can be stated in the form of empirical propositions that can be tested in the field.

Finally, a number of directions in which this and other simulation models might be developed suggest themselves. The predisposition phase of the model could be investigated to see whether including personal characteristics of representatives as predisposing effects would increase the predictability of roll-call votes. The communications phase of the model could be reformulated in two ways. First, a number of variables could be added to affect conversation probabilities, and second, the communication process could be cycled to allow for a diffusion of influence whereby those whose predispositions have been changed as a result of interactions with colleagues could interact with other colleagues as influencers on the basis of their newly acquired predispositions.

What is perhaps most significant for the model's future research possibilities is the relative similarity of state legislatures to the Congress. The model should be employed in simulations of roll-call voting in state legislatures as well as other sessions in the House to develop it to the point where it simulates legislative voting in a broader sense. In this way, one could enhance the organizing power of a theoretical formulation, the potential of which we have just begun to explore.

Appendixes

A. The Program*

```
    PROGRAM SLP (SIMULATED LEGISLATIVE PROCESSES)          001
    DIMENSION ID (435), ISTAT(435), IREG(435), ICON(435,9),
      ICOM(435,3),                                         002
   1ILEAD(435),JREG(5),JCON(9),JCOM(3),PRED(435),JSTAT(4),
      KLEAD(435),                                          003
   2IRANK(435,3),IWHIP(435),JSPON(15),ISFN(435),IPAR(435),
      IFED(435),                                           004
   3JFED(435),KCOM(15),KVOTE(535),ISCORE(435),JSCORE(435), 005
   4PARRT(2),REGRT(5),STATRT(50),CONRT(4,9),SENRT(3),      006
   5PARSUM(2),STATSUM(50),REGSUM(5),CONSUM(4,9),SENSUM(3)  007
    TYPE INTEGER SUMYES, SUMNO, SUMDET, SUMCON, SUMNVOTE,
      SUMACON                                              008
    CALL RANFSET (TIMEF(0,0))                              009
    DO 187 I=1,435                                         010
    ISCORE(I)=0                                            011
    JSCORE(I)=0                                            012
187 CONTINUE                                               013
C READ IN ATTRIBUTES OF CONGRESSMEN
C ID=IDENTIFICATION, IPAR=PARTY, ISTAT=STATE, IREG=REGION
C ICON=CONSTITUENCY, ILEAD=LEADERSHIP, ICOM=COMMITTEE
C ISEN=SENIORITY, KLEAD=LEADERSHIP POSITION
```

*This program was written by Michael Shapiro. The computer language is Fortran IV and the simulation runs were processed on the CDC 3400 at Northwestern University's Vogelback Computational Center.

```
C IRANK=COMMITTEE RANK, IWHIP=REGIONAL WHIP
C IFED=VOTES FOR FEDERAL ROLE, JFED=TIMES VOTING ON SUCH
    ISSUES
      READ (60,1)(ID(1),IPAR(1),ISTAT(1),IREG(1),(ICON(I,J),J=1,9),    014
     1ILEAD(I),(ICOM(I,J),J=1,3),ISEN(I),KLEAD(I),(IRANK(I,J),
       J=1,3),                                                          015
     2IWHIP(I),IFED(I),JFED(I),I=1,435)                                 016
    1 FORMAT (13,11,12,11,911,312,11,3X,11,311,12,12,12)                017
C READ IN BILLS
C JPAR=PARTY, JSTAT=STATE, JREG=REGION, JCON=CONSTITUENCY
C JCOM=COMMITTEE, KCOM=MINORITY REPORT FROM COMMITTEE
C JSPON=SPONSORSHIP, JPARP=PRESIDENTS PARTY
C JSTATP=PRESIDENTS STATE, JREGP=PRESIDENTS REGION
C KFED=FEDERAL ROLE CONSEQUENCES, KVOTE=ACTUAL VOTES
        OF EACH REPRESENTATIVE
    2 READ (60,3) (JPAR,(JSTAT(I),I=1,4),(JREG(I),I=1,5),
        (JCON(I),I=1,9)                                                 018
     1,(JCOM(I),I=1,3),(KCOM(I),I=1,15),(JSPON(I),I=1,15),
        JPARP,JSTATP,                                                   019
     2JREGP,KFED,(KVOTE(I),I=1,435)                                     020
    3 FORMAT(I1,4I2,5I2,9I1,3I2,15I3/15I3,I1,I2,I1/8OI1/8OI1/8OI1/      021
    1    8OI1/8OI1/35I1)                                                022
      SUMYES=0 $ SUMNO=0 $ SUMNVOTE=0 $ SUMDET=0 $
        SUMVOTE=0 $ SUMRIGHT=0                                          023
      DO 503 I=1,2                                                      024
      PARSUM(I)=0                                                       025
      PARRT(I)=0                                                        026
  503 CONTINUE                                                          027
      DO 502 I=1,9                                                      028
      DO 502 J=1,4                                                      029
      CONSUM(J,I)=0                                                     030
      CONRT(J,I)=0                                                      031
  502 CONTINUE                                                          032
      DO 504 I=1,50                                                     033
      STATSUM(I)=0                                                      034
      STATRT(I)=0                                                       035
  504 CONTINUE                                                          036
      DO 505 I=1,5                                                      037
      REGSUM(I)=0                                                       038
      REGRT(I)=0                                                        039
  505 CONTINUE                                                          040
      DO 506 I=1,3                                                      041
      SENSUM(I)=0                                                       042
      SENRT(I)=0                                                        043
  506 CONTINUE                                                          044
      IF (JPAR.GT.4)4,5                                                 045
```

```
      4 GO TO 200                                    046
C BEGIN VOTE CALCULATION PROCESS
      5 DO 359 IVOTE=1,435                           047
        PRED(IVOTE)=0.                               048
        IF(KFED.LT.1)340,293                         049
    293 IF(JFED(IVOTE).LT.10)340,341                 050
    341 RFED=IFED(IVOTE)                             051
        SFED=JFED(IVOTE)                             052
        RECALL=RFED/SFED                             053
        IF (RECALL.GT..85)320,351                    054
    320 IF(KFED.EQ.1)342,343                         055
    342 PRED(IVOTE)=PRED(IVOTE)+2.                    056
        GO TO 340                                    057
    343 PRED(IVOTE)=PRED(IVOTE)-2.                    058
        GO TO 340                                    059
    351 IF(RECALL.GT..65)352,353                     060
    352 IF(KFED.EQ.1)354,355                         061
    354 PRED(IVOTE)=PRED(IVOTE)+1.                    062
        GO TO 340                                    063
    355 PRED(IVOTE)=PRED(IVOTE)-1.                    064
        GO TO 340                                    065
    353 IF(RECALL.LT..15)356,321                     066
    356 IF(KFED.EQ.2)357,358                         067
    357 PRED(IVOTE)=PRED(IVOTE)+2.                    068
        GO TO 340                                    069
    358 PRED(IVOTE)=PRED(IVOTE)-2.                    070
        GO TO 340                                    071
    321 IF(RECALL.LT..35)322,340                     072
    322 IF(KFED.EQ.2)344,345                         073
    344 PRED(IVOTE)=PRED(IVOTE)+1.                    074
        GO TO 340                                    075
    345 PRED(IVOTE)=PRED(IVOTE)-1.                    076
    340 IF (IPAR(IVOTE).EQ.JPAR)6,7                   077
      6 PRED(IVOTE)=PRED(IVOTE)+1.                    078
        GO TO 10                                     079
      7 GO TO (8,8,9,10),JPAR                         080
      8 PRED(IVOTE)=PRED(IVOTE)-1.                    081
        GO TO 10                                     082
      9 PRED(IVOTE)=PRED(IVOTE)+1.                    083
     10 DO 300 I=1,15                                084
        IF (ID(IVOTE).EQ.JSPON(I))297,300            085
    297 PRED(IVOTE)=PRED(IVOTE)+2.                    086
    300 CONTINUE                                      087
    299 DO 12 I=1,4                                   088
        IF (ISTAT(IVOTE).EQ.JSTAT(I))11,12           089
     11 PRED(IVOTE)=PRED(IVOTE)+1.                    090
```

```
12 CONTINUE                                              091
   DO 16 I=1,5                                           092
   IF(IREG(IVOTE).EQ.JREG(I))13,14                       093
13 PRED(IVOTE)=PRED(IVOTE)+1.                            094
   GO TO 16                                              095
14 IF(JREG(I)-IREG(IVOTE).EQ.10)15,16                    096
15 PRED(IVOTE)=PRED(IVOTE)-1.                            097
16 CONTINUE                                              098
   ISAL=0                                                099
   DO 20 I=1,9                                           100
   IF (ICON(IVOTE,I).EQ.JCON(I))17,18                    101
17 ISAL=ISAL+1                                           102
   GO TO 20                                              103
18 IF (ICON(IVOTE,I)+5.EQ.JCON(I))19,20                  104
19 ISAL=ISAL-1                                           105
20 CONTINUE                                              106
   IF (ISAL)21,22,23                                     107
21 PRED(IVOTE)=PRED(IVOTE)-1.                            108
   IF(ICON(IVOTE,9).EQ.1)178,179                         109
178 PRED(IVOTE)=PRED(IVOTE)-1.                           110
179 GO TO 22                                             111
23 PRED(IVOTE)=PRED(IVOTE)+1.                            112
   IF(ICON(IVOTE,9).EQ.1)180,22                          113
180 PRED(IVOTE)=PRED(IVOTE)+1.                           114
22 CONTINUE                                              115
   GO TO (25,30,31,34),JPAR                              116
25 IF (ILEAD(IVOTE).EQ.1.OR.ILEAD(IVOTE).EQ.2.OR.
      ILEAD(IVOTE).EQ.4)                                 117
  1 26,27                                                118
26 PRED(IVOTE)=PRED(IVOTE)+1.                            119
   GO TO 34                                              120
27 IF(ILEAD(IVOTE).EQ.3.OR.ILEAD(IVOTE).EQ.5)28,29       121
28 PRED(IVOTE)=PRED(IVOTE)-1.                            122
29 GO TO 34                                              123
30 IF(ILEAD(IVOTE).EQ.3.OR.ILEAD(IVOTE).EQ.5)26,32       124
31 IF(ILEAD(IVOTE).GE.1)26,34                            125
32 IF(ILEAD(IVOTE).EQ.1.OR.ILEAD(IVOTE).EQ.2.OR.
      ILEAD(IVOTE).EQ.4)                                 126
  133,34                                                 127
33 PRED(IVOTE)=PRED(IVOTE)=1.                            128
34 DO 36 I=1,3                                           129
   DO 36 J=1,3                                           130
   IF (ICOM(IVOTE,I).EQ.JCOM(J))35,36                    131
35 PRED(IVOTE)=PRED(IVOTE)+1.                            132
36 CONTINUE                                              133
   DO 359 I=1,15                                         134
```

```
        IF(ID(IVOTE).EQ.KCOM(I))360,359                          135
360 PRED(IVOTE)=PRED(IVOTE)-2.                                   136
359 CONTINUE                                                     137
C ASSESS THE STRENGTH OF THE PREDISPOSITIONS
        DO 350  IVOTE=1,435                                      138
        IF(KVOTE(IVOTE).EQ.1.OR.KVOTE(IVOTE).EQ.2)181,350        139
181 SUMVOTE=SUMVOTE+1                                            140
        MA=IPAR(IVOTE)                                           141
        MB=ISTAT(IVOTE)                                          142
        MC=IREG(IVOTE)                                           143
        DO 500  I=1,9                                            144
        MD=ICON(IVOTE,I)                                         145
        CONSUM(MD,I)=CONSUM(MD,I)+1                              146
500 CONTINUE                                                     147
        ME=ISEN(IVOTE)                                           148
        PARSUM(MA)=PARSUM(MA)+1                                  149
        STATSUM(MB)=STATSUM(MB)+1                                150
        REGSUM(MC)=REGSUM(MC)+1                                  151
        SENSUM(ME)=SENSUM(ME)+1                                  152
        JFED(IVOTE)=JFED(IVOTE)+1                                153
        IF (PRED(IVOTE).GE.2.)37,38                              154
 37 JVOTE=1                                                      155
        SUMYES=SUMYES+1                                          156
        SUMDET=SUMDET+1                                          157
        IF(JVOTE.EQ.KVOTE(IVOTE))182,183                         158
182 SUMRIGHT=SUMRIGHT+1                                          159
        PARRT(MA)=PARRT(MA)+1                                    160
        STATRT(MB)=STATRT(MB)+1                                  161
        REGRT(MC)=REGRT(MC)+1                                    162
        DO 501  I=1,9                                            163
        MD=ICON(IVOTE,I)                                         164
        CONRT(MD,I)=CONRT(MD,I)+1                                165
501 CONTINUE                                                     166
        SENRT(ME)=SENRT(ME)+1                                    167
        IF(KFED.EQ.1)400,402                                     168
400 IFED(IVOTE)=IFED(IVOTE)+1                                    169
        ISCORE(IVOTE)=ISCORE(IVOTE)+1                            170
        JSCORE(IVOTE)=JSCORE(IVOTE)+1                            171
        GO TO 402                                                172
183 IF(KFED.EQ.2)401,602                                         173
401 IFED(IVOTE)=IFED(IVOTE)+1                                    174
        ISCORE(IVOTE)=ISCORE(IVOTE)+1                            175
602 JSCORE(IVOTE)=JSCORE(IVOTE)+1                                176
402 WRITE (61,39) ID(IVOTE),PRED(IVOTE),JVOTE                    177
 39 FORMAT (15X,* NUMBER *,I3,2X,* PRED *,F5.2,2X,I2)            178
        GO TO 350                                                179
```

```
 38 IF (PRED(IVOTE).LE.−2.)40,42                         180
 40 JVOTE=2                                              181
    SUMNO=SUMNO+1                                        182
    SUMDET=SUMDET+1                                      183
    IF(JVOTE.EQ.KVOTE(IVOTE))184,185                     184
184 SUMRIGHT=SUMRIGHT+1                                  185
    PARRT(MA)=PARRT(MA)+1                                186
    STATRT(MB)=STATRT(MB)+1                              187
    REGRT(MC)=REGRT(MC)+1                                188
    DO 507 I=1,9                                         189
    MD=ICON(IVOTE,I)                                     190
    CONRT(MD,I)=CONRT(MD,I)+1                            191
507 CONTINUE                                             192
    SENRT(ME)=SENRT(ME)+1                                193
    IF(KFED.EQ.2)403,186                                 194
403 IFED(IVOTE)=IFED(IVOTE)+1                            195
    JSCORE(IVOTE)=JSCORE(IVOTE)+1                        196
    ISCORE(IVOTE)=ISCORE(IVOTE)+1                        197
    GO TO 186                                            198
185 IF(KFED.EQ.1) 404,686                                199
404 IFED(IVOTE)=IFED(IVOTE)+1                            200
    ISCORE(IVOTE)=ISCORE(IVOTE)+1                        201
686 JSCORE(IVOTE)=JSCORE(IVOTE)+1                        202
186 WRITE (61,39) ID(IVOTE),PRED(IVOTE),JVOTE            203
    GO TO 350                                            204
C BEGIN THE COMMUNICATION PROCESS
 42 SUMCOM=0                                             205
    SUMACOM=0                                            206
    SUMINF=0                                             207
    IF (JPARP.GT.0)250,251                               208
250 PROB=0.                                              209
    IF (IPAR(IVOTE).EQ.JPARP)301, 302                    210
301 PROB=PROB+.04                                        211
    GO TO 307                                            212
302 PROB=PROB+.01                                        213
307 IF (ISTAT(IVOTE).EQ.JSTATP)303,304                   214
303 PROB=PROB+.2                                         215
    GO TO 306                                            216
304 IF (IREG(IVOTE).EQ.JREGP)305,306                     217
305 PROB=PROB+.O5                                        218
306 Y=RANF(−1)                                           219
    IF(Y.LE.PROB)308,251                                 220
308 IF(JPAR.EQ.3.OR.JPAR.EQ.JPARP)323,324                221
323 SUMINF=SUMINF+2.                                     222
    GO TO 329                                            223
324 SUMINF=SUMINF−2.                                     224
```

```
329 SUMCOM=SUMCOM+1                                                     225
    SUMACOM=SUMACOM+1                                                   226
251 DO 125 ITALK=1,435                                                  227
    PROB=0.                                                             228
    IF (IVOTE.EQ.ITALK)43,44                                           229
 43 GO TO 125                                                           230
 44 IF(ILEAD(IVOTE).LT.9.AND.ILEAD(IVOTE).GT.0)47,76                    231
 47 IF (ILEAD(IVOTE).EQ.2.AND.ILEAD(ITALK).EQ.I.OR.                     232
       ILEAD(IVOTE).EQ.1.                                              233
   1AND.ILEAD(ITALK).EQ.2)49,50                                        234
 49 PROB=.9                                                            235
    GO TO 115                                                          236
 50 IF(ILEAD(IVOTE).EQ.2.AND.ILEAD(ITALK).EQ.3.
       OR.ILEAD(IVOTE).EQ.3.                                           237
   1AND.ILEAD(ITALK).EQ.2)51,52                                        238
 51 PROB=.3                                                            239
    GO TO 115                                                          240
 52 IF(ILEAD(IVOTE).EQ.2.AND.KLEAD(ITALK).EQ.1.OR.                     241
       KLEAD(IVOTE).EQ.1.                                              242
   1AND.ILEAD(ITALK).EQ.2)53,54                                        243
 53 PROB=.8                                                            244
    GO TO 115                                                          245
 54 IF(ILEAD(IVOTE).EQ.1.AND.ILEAD(ITALK).EQ.3.
       OR.ILEAD(IVOTE).EQ.3.                                           246
   1AND.ILEAD(ITALK).EQ.1)55,56                                        247
 55 PROB=.3                                                            248
    GO TO 115                                                          249
 56 IF(ILEAD(IVOTE).EQ.1.AND.KLEAD(ITALK).EQ.1.
       OR.KLEAD(IVOTE).EQ.1.                                           250
   1AND.ILEAD(ITALK).EQ.1)57,58                                        251
 57 PROB=.7                                                            252
    GO TO 115                                                          253
 58 IF(ILEAD(IVOTE),EQ,1,AND,ILEAD(ITALK).EQ.4.
       OR.ILEAD(IVOTE).EQ.4.                                           254
   1AND.ILEAD(ITALK).EQ.1)59,60                                        255
 59 PROB=.3                                                            256
    GO TO 115                                                          257
 60 IF(ILEAD(IVOTE).EQ.2.AND.KLEAD(ITALK).EQ.4.
       OR.ILEAD(IVOTE).EQ.4.                                           258
   1AND.ILEAD(ITALK).EQ.2)61,62                                        259
 61 PROB=.3                                                            260
    GO TO 115                                                          261
 62 IF(KLEAD(IVOTE).EQ.1.AND.ILEAD(ITALK).EQ.4.
       OR.ILEAD(IVOTE).EQ.4.                                           262
   1AND.KLEAD(ITALK).EQ.1)63,64                                        263
 63 PROB=.8                                                            264
```

```
      GO TO 115                                                  265
 64 IF(ILEAD(IVOTE).EQ.4.AND.ILEAD(ITALK).EQ.4)65,66            266
 65 PROB=.6                                                      267
      GO TO 115                                                  268
 66 IF(ILEAD(IVOTE).EQ.3.AND.KLEAD(ITALK).EQ.3.
         OR.KLEAD(IVOTE).EQ.3.                                  269
    1AND.ILEAD(ITALK).EQ.3)67,68                                270
 67 PROB=.7                                                      271
      GO TO 115                                                  272
 68 IF(ILEAD(IVOTE).EQ.3.AND.ILEAD(ITALK).EQ.5.OR.
         ILEAD(IVOTE).EQ.5.                                     273
    1AND.ILEAD(ITALK).EQ.3)69,70                                274
 69 PROB=.2                                                      275
      GO TO 115                                                  276
 70 IF(KLEAD(IVOTE).EQ.3.AND.ILEAD(ITALK).EQ.5.
         OR.ILEAD(IVOTE).EQ.5.                                  277
    1AND.KLEAD(ITALK).EQ.3)71,72                                278
 71 PROB=.6                                                      279
      GO TO 115                                                  280
 72 IF(ILEAD(IVOTE).EQ.5.AND.ILEAD(ITALK).EQ.5)73,74            281
 73 PROB=.4                                                      282
      GO TO 115                                                  283
 74 (IF(ILEAD(IVOTE).EQ.1.AND.KLEAD(ITALK).EQ.3.
         OR.KLEAD(IVOTE).EQ.3.                                  284
    1AND.ILEAD(ITALK).EQ.1)75,76                                285
 75 PROB=.2                                                      286
      GO TO 115                                                  287
 76 IF(IPAR(IVOTE).EQ.IPAR(ITALK))77,78                         288
 77 PROB=PROB+.04                                                289
      IF(ILEAD(ITALK).EQ.4.OR.ILEAD(ITALK).EQ.5.AND
         IWHIP(IVOTE).EQ.                                       290
    1IWHIP(ITALK))201,202                                       291
201 PROB=.9                                                      292
      GO TO 115                                                  293
 78 PROB=PROB+.01                                                294
202 IF(ISTAT(IVOTE).EQ.ISTAT(ITALK))79,80                       295
 79 PROB=PROB+.3                                                 296
      GO TO 82                                                   297
 80 IF(IREG(IVOTE).EQ.IREG(ITALK))81,82                         298
 81 PROB=PROB+.05                                                299
 82 DO 83 I=1,3                                                  300
      IF(ICON(IVOTE,I).EQ.ICON(ITALK,I))83,85                   301
 83 CONTINUE                                                     302
      PROB=PROB+.01                                              303
 85 DO 87 I=1,3                                                  304
      DO 87 J=1,3                                                305
```

```
      IF(ICOM(IVOTE,I).GT.0.AND.ICOM(IVOTE,I).
         EQ.ICOM(ITALK,J))86,87                              306
   86 PROB=PROB+.05                                          307
      GO TO 88                                               308
   87 CONTINUE                                               309
   88 IF(ILEAD(ITALK).LT.4.OR.ILEAD(ITALK).GT.5)89,90        310
   89 IF(ISEN(IVOTE),EQ.ISEN(ITALK))91,90                    311
   91 PROB=PROB+.02                                          312
   90 IF(ILEAD(ITALK).EQ.9)92,93                             313
   92 DO 95 I=1,3                                            314
      IF(ICOM(ITALK,1).EQ.JCOM(I).AND.IPAR(IVOTE).
         EQ.IPAR(ITALK))94,95                                315
   94 PROB=PROB+.02                                          316
      GO TO 93                                               317
   95 CONTINUE                                               318
   93 IF (IPAR(IVOTE).EQ.IPAR(ITALK))96,115                  319
   96 DO 99 I = 1,3                                          320
      DO 99 J= 1,3                                           321
      DO 99 K = 1,3                                          322
      IF (ICOM(ITALK,I).EQ.JCOM(J)) 98,99                    323
   98 IF (IRANK(K).EQ.1)100,101                              324
  100 PROB= PROB +.03                                        325
      GO TO 99                                               326
  101 PROB = PROB +.01                                       327
   99 CONTINUE                                               328
   97 IF (ILEAD(ITALK).EQ.1)102,103                          329
  102 PROB=PROB+.03                                          330
      GO TO 115                                              331
  103 IF (ILEAD(ITALK).EQ.2)104,105                          332
  104 PROB =   PROB +.04                                     333
      GO TO 115                                              334
  105 IF (KLEAD(ITALK).EQ.1)106,107                          335
  106 PROB = PROB + .02                                      336
      GO TO 115                                              337
  107 IF (KLEAD(ITALK).EQ.2)108,109                          338
  108 PROB = PROB + .01                                      339
      GO TO 115                                              340
  109 IF(ILEAD(ITALK).EQ.3)110,111                           341
  110 PROB = PROB + .03                                      342
      GO TO 115                                              343
  111 IF (KLEAD(ITALK).EQ.3)112,113                          344
  112 PROB = PROB + .015                                     345
      GO TO 115                                              346
  113 IF (KLEAD(ITALK).EQ.4) 114,115                         347
  114 PROB = PROB + .007                                     348
C CALL RANDOM NUMBER
```

```
115 Y = RANF(−1)                                             349
    (F(Y.LE.PROB)116,125                                     350
116 SUMACOM=SUMACOM+1                                        351
117 SUMINF=SUMINF+PRED(ITALK)                                352
    SUMCON=SUMCOM+1                                          353
125 CONTINUE                                                 354
    PREDLAST=(SUMINF/SUMCOM+PRED(IVOTE))/2.                  355
    IF(PREDLAST.GT.0.)118,119                                356
118 JVOTE=1                                                  357
    SUMYES = SUMYES +1                                       358
    IF(JVOTE.EQ.KVOTE(IVOTE))188,189                         359
188 SUMRIGHT=SUMRIGHT+1                                      360
    PARRT(MA)=PARRT(MA)+1                                    361
    STATRT(MB)=STATRT(MB)+1                                  362
    REGRT(MC)=REGRT(MC)+1                                    363
    DO508I=1,9                                               364
    MD=ICON(IVOTE,I)                                         365
    CONRT(MD,I)=CONRT(MD,I)+1                                366
508 CONTINUE                                                 367
    SENRT(ME)=SENRT(ME)+1                                    368
    IF(KFED.EQ.1)405,407                                     369
405 IFED(IVOTE)=IFED(IVOTE)+1                                370
    JSCORE(IVOTE)=JSCORE(IVOTE)+1                            371
    ISCORE(IVOTE)=ISCORE(IVOTE)+1                            372
    GO TO 407                                                373
189 IF(KFED.EQ.2)406,607                                     374
406 IFED(IVOTE)=IFED(IVOTE)+1                                375
    ISCORE(IVOTE)=ISCORE(IVOTE)+1                            376
607 JSCORE(IVOTE)=JSCORE(IVOTE)+1                            377
407 WRITE (61,122) ID(IVOTE),PRED(IVOTE),JVOTE,SUMACOM       378
122 FORMAT (15X,*NUMBER *,I3,* PRED *,F5.2,2X,I2,2X,I5)       379
    GO TO 350                                                380
119 IF(PREDLAST.LT.0.)120,121                                381
120 JVOTE=2                                                  382
    SUMNO = SUMNO + 1                                        383
    IF(JVOTE.EQ.KVOTE(IVOTE))190,191                         384
190 SUMRIGHT=SUMRIGHT+1                                      385
    PARRT(MA)=PARRT(MA)+1                                    386
    STATRT(MB)=STATRT(MB)+1                                  387
    REGRT(MC)=REGRT(MC)+1                                    388
    DO509I=1,9                                               389
    MD=ICON(IVOTE,I)                                         390
    CONRT(MD,I)=CONRT(MD,I)+1                                391
509 CONTINUE                                                 392
    SENRT(ME)=SENRT(ME)+1                                    393
    IF(KFED.EQ.2)408,192                                     394
```

```
408 IFED(IVOTE)=IFED(IVOTE)+1                                          395
    ISCORE(IVOTE)=ISCORE(IVOTE)+1                                      396
    JSCORE(IVOTE)=JSCORE(IVOTE)+1                                      397
    GO TO 192                                                          398
191 IF(KFED.EQ.1)409,692                                               399
409 IFED(IVOTE)=IFED(IVOTE)+1                                          400
    ISCORE(IVOTE)=ISCORE(IVOTE)+1                                      401
692 JSCORE(IVOTE)=JSCORE(IVOTE)+1                                      402
192 WRITE (61,122) ID(IVOTE),PRED(IVOTE),JVOTE,SUMACOM                 403
    GO TO 350                                                          404
121 JVOTE = 6HNOVOTE                                                   405
    SUMNVOTE = SUMNVOTE + 1                                            406
    GO TO (410,411),KFED                                               407
410 IF(KVOTE(IVOTE).EQ.1)412,413                                       408
412 IFED(IVOTE)=IFED(IVOTE)+1                                          409
    ISCORE(IVOTE)=ISCORE(IVOTE)+1                                      410
    GO TO 413                                                          411
411 IF(KVOTE(IVOTE).EQ.2)414,413                                       412
414 IFED(IVOTE)=IFED(IVOTE)+1                                          413
    ISCORE(IVOTE)=ISCORE(IVOTE)+1                                      414
413 WRITE (61,122) ID(IVOTE),PRED(IVOTE),JVOTE,SUMACOM                 415
350 CONTINUE                                                           416
    DO 510 I=1,2                                                       417
    PROP=PARRT(I)/PARSUM(I)                                            418
    WRITE(61,511) I,PROP                                               419
511 FORMAT (15X,* PARTY *,I1,* PROPORTION RIGHT *,F5.3)                420
510 CONTINUE                                                           421
    DO 512 I=1,50                                                      422
    PROP=STATRT(I)/STATSUM(I)                                          423
    WRITE(61,513) I,PROP                                               424
513 FORMAT(15X,* STATE *,I2,* PROPORTION RIGHT *,F5.3)                 425
512 CONTINUE                                                           426
    DO 514 I=1,5                                                       427
    PROP=REGRT(I)/REGSUM(I)                                            428
    WRITE(61,515) I,PROP                                               429
515 FORMAT(15X,* REGION *,I1,* PROPORTION RIGHT *,F5.3)                430
514 CONTINUE                                                           431
    DO 516 I=1,3                                                       432
    PROP=SENRT(I)/SENSUM(I)                                            433
    WRITE(61,517) I,PROP                                               434
517 FORMAT(15X,* SENIORITY *,I1,* PROPORTION RIGHT *,F5.3)             435
516 CONTINUE                                                           436
    DO 518 I=1,9                                                       437
    DO 518 J=1,4                                                       438
    PROP=CONRT(J,I)/CONSUM(J,I)                                        439
    WRITE(61,519) I,J,PROP                                             440
```

```
519 FORMAT(15X,* VARIABLE *,I1,* FACTOR *,I1,* PROPORTION        441
    RIGHT *,1F5,3)                                               442
518 CONTINUE                                                     443
    PRIGHT=SUMRIGHT/SUMVOTE                                      444
    WRITE (61,126) SUMYES, SUMNO, SUMNVOTE, SUMDET,PRIGHT        445
126 FORMAT 15X,*SUMYES *,I5,* SUMNO *,I5,* SUMNOVOTE *,I5,       446
    1*SUMDETERMINED*,I5,* PERCENT RIGHT *,F5.2)                  447
    GO TO 2                                                      448
200 DO 702 I=1,435                                               449
    PUNCH 701,IPAR(I),ISTAT(I),IREG(I),ICON(I,J),J=1,9),ISEN(I), 450
    1ISCORE(I),JSCORE(I)                                         451
701 FORMAT (5X,I1,I2,I1,9I1,I1,2I2)                              452
702 CONTINUE                                                     453
    STOP                                                         454
    END                                                         455
```

B. SUMMARY OF PROPOSITIONS

All the propositions in the text are listed below. The previous discussion indicated that propositions were used (1) in writing the computer program, and (2) in guiding coding decisions concerning each bill. Those propositions actually built into the program are indexed to the Record Number of each computer statement listed in Appendix A. Those propositions that helped guide coding decisions on bills input are identified by the notation "C.G." Fifty-one of the 69 propositions discussed in the text were used in writing the program and in making coding decisions. The propositions that were not utilized suggest several possible extensions of the model.

	Computer Program
Proposition	*Record Numbers*
1. Party affiliation is highly related to roll-call voting (p. 25).	77–83
2. Party loyalty is composed of loyalty to the organization and loyalty to the ideology (p. 25).	
3. Democrats tend to be more loyal to the party organization than Republicans (p. 25).	
4. Republicans tend to be more loyal to the party ideology than Democrats (p. 25).	
5. In Congress, party loyalty tends to be stronger among members of the majority than among members of the minority (p. 25).	210–214

6. Party affiliation commands different degrees of loyalty across different issues (p. 25). C.G.

7. Party loyalty tends to be increased when party is supported by salient factors, such as region and constituency, and is decreased when opposed by salient audiences (p. 25). 47–176

8. Party leaders tend to be more loyal to the party organization and ideology than rank and file members (p. 25). 116–128

9. Political and demographic characteristics of legislative districts are related to roll call behavior (p. 30). 99–114

10. Inter-party competitiveness in state legislatures tends to be related to fewer party votes and inhibits legislators from taking extreme ideological positions (p. 30).

11. Inter-party competitiveness in the House of Representatives does not seem to be related to party voting but does decrease the tendency for representatives to take extreme ideological positions (p. 30). 113–114

12. Legislative districts atypical of party strength tend to produce less party loyalty at the roll-call stage (p. 30). 77–83
 99–114

13. The relationship between constituency and roll-call voting tends to be issue specific: the areas of greatest influence are on affairs within the district and the weakest influence is on affairs outside the district (p. 30). C.G.

14. Party dominance tends to be related to the demographic variables of owner-occupied housing, population per square mile, percent non-white, and percent urban (p. 30).

15. The sectional base of a congressman tends to be related to his roll-call voting (p. 33). 93–98

16. As party unity decreases on roll calls within the House of Representatives cohesion within regional groups tends to increase (p. 33). 77–83
 93–98

17. Intra-party conflict within the Democrat party in the House of Representatives tends to be associated with cleavage between northern and southern representatives (p. 33). C.G.

18. Intra-party conflict within the Republican party tends to be less consistent and less associated with region than within the Democratic party (p. 33). C.G.

19. Intra-party conflict within the Republican party exists between coastal and midwestern congressmen (p. 33). C.G.

20. As the relationship between party and votes on foreign aid has declined, the relationship between region and foreign aid voting has increased (p. 33). C.G.

21. The political predispositions or ideologies of congressmen are related to roll-call voting even when the effects
of party, region, and constituency are controlled (p. 35).   49–76
22. Congressmen differentially perceive a wide range of conflict in a legislature: longer legislative service, more
formal education and less geographic isolation are related
to viewing legislative conflict in complex terms (p. 35).
23. Legislators with a narrow perception of legislative conflict tend to be less aware of interest group activity and
tend to be high on ideological loyalty to the party (p. 35).
24. Legislators tend to be very consistent in their roll-call
votes from one Congressional session to the next (p. 35).   49–76
25. Frequency of communication is higher among majority
than among minority members in a legislature (p. 38).
26. Frequency of communication is higher among experi-
enced members than among neophytes (p. 39).   319–327
27. There tends to be a high, positive relationship between   332–348
high influencers and high interactors (p. 39).   355
28. State delegations tend to have a higher than average
amount of interaction and voting cohesion in the House
of Representatives (p. 39).   295–296
29. Friendship groups do not tend to perform an integrating
function in a legislature (p. 39).
30. Legislative norms focus on: (1) apprenticeship, (2) legislative work, (3) specialization, (4) courtesy, (5) reciprocity, and (6) institutional patriotism (p. 42).
31. Legislative norms perform the functions of (1) promoting
group cohesion and solidarity, (2) increasing the predictability of legislative behavior, (3) channelling and restraining conflict, and (4) expediting legislative business
(p. 42).
32. Legislators tend toward high agreement on legislative
norms (p. 42).
33. There is a direct, positive relationship between conformity to legislative norms and legislative effectiveness (p. 42).
34. Legislators expect their leaders to focus issues and resolve
conflict by the dissemination of information (p. 42).
35. Legislators expect their leaders to administer the system
so that it will be stable and predictable (p. 42).
36. Norms operative in a legislative committee are partially
adopted from the norms of the legislature as a whole
(p. 42).
37. The integration of legislative committees is related to:
(1) the existence of a well-articulated and established set

of goals, (2) the nature of the committee's subject matter, (3) the legislative orientation of its members, (4) the attractiveness of the committee for its members, and (5) the stability of its membership (p. 43).

38. Well integrated committees give voting cues to members that tend to be followed at the roll-call stage (p. 43).   129–132   C.G.

39. All legislative committees do not provide cues that produce high cohesion among their members on roll-call votes (p. 43).   C.G.

40. Voting cohesion among committee members tends to be inversely correlated with voting among members of the legislative party (p. 43).   77–83   129–132

41. Persons who hold extreme positions are less susceptible to counter-influences than are individuals who hold moderate positions (p. 52).   138–204

42. When pressures salient to political decision-making are convergent, decisions tend to be made earlier than when salient pressures conflict (p. 56).   138–204

43. Persons with intense preferences who make early voting decisions are more likely to be influencers and those who postpone voting decisions tend to be targets of influence (p. 56).   355

44. Individuals with more extreme attitude positions are less susceptible to influence than individuals with less extreme attitude positions (p. 66).   138–204

45. A legislator with two or more pressures such as party and constituency influencing his vote in the same direction is unlikely to be susceptible to further influence concerning his vote (p. 66).   138–204

46. The president communicates with legislators in order to influence the passage of his legislative programs (p. 69).   205–227

47. The president communicates more frequently with members of his own party than with opposition party members. (p. 71).   210–214

48. The president communicates more frequently with representatives from his home state than with other representatives (p. 71).   215–216

49. The president communicates more frequently with representatives from his region of the country than with other representatives (p. 71).   218–219

50. The formal leadership in the House tends to correspond closely to the actual leadership (p. 74).   232–286   290–292   313–348

51. The leadership in the House interacts frequently (p. 74).   332–348

52. The Speaker of the House and the House Majority Leader
consult each other frequently (p. 74).   234–236

53. The relationship between the Speaker and Majority
Leader is closer than that between either of them and
the minority leaders (p. 74).   234–240

54. Frequent interactions occur between the whips and the   262–263
whip organization (p. 74).   277–278

55. Frequent interactions occur between the whips, whip
organizations, and other elected leaders (p. 74).   250–286

56. House leaders are involved in twice as many communicative interactions as rank and file members (p. 75). 205–356

57. A representative is contacted by his regional whip before
most roll calls (p. 75).   290–292

58. Representatives speak to an average of 25 to 30 colleagues
before a roll call (p. 75).   205–356

59. A representative tends to have four times as many communicative interactions with members of his own party as
with members of the opposition (p. 77).   288–294

60. State delegations are important sources of communication
for representatives (p. 77).   295–296

61. Representatives communicate disproportionately with
colleagues from their region (p. 77).   298–299

62. Similarity of constituency is a source of communication
among representatives (p. 78).   300–303

63. Representatives communicate with colleagues who share
their committee assignments (p. 78).   304–309

64. Communication among representatives takes place disproportionately within seniority groupings (p. 78). 311–312

65. The committee chairmen and high ranking members receive a disproportionate share of communications (p. 80). 313–327

66. The higher the rank of the elected leader, the more the
communications in which he engages (p. 80).   332–348

67. Elected leaders in the majority party engage in more
communications than those in the minority party (p. 80). 332–348

68. A representative who communicates on a bill changes his
original predisposition toward the bill to a position halfway between his original predisposition and the average
one that he confronts in his communications with the
president and his colleagues (p. 82).   355

Bibliography

Abelson, R. P., and Rosenberg, M. J. Symbolic psychologic: A model of attitudinal cognition, *Behavioral science*, 3, 1958, 1–13.

Abelson, R. P. Modes of resolution of belief dilemmas, *Journal of conflict resolution*, 3, 1959, 343–352.

Abelson, R. P. The use of surveys in simulations, *Public opinion quarterly*, 26, 1962, 485–486.

Abelson, R. P. Computer simulation of hot cognition. In S. Tomkins and S. Messick, eds., *Computer simulation of personality*. New York: Wiley, 1963.

Abelson, R. P., and Bernstein, A. A computer simulation model of community referendum controversies, *Public opinion quarterly*, 27, 1963, 93–122.

Abelson, R. P., and Carroll, J. D. Computer simulation of individual belief systems, *American behavioral scientist*, 8, 1965, 24–30.

Abelson, R. P. Simulation of social behavior. In G. Lindzey and E. Aronson, eds., *Handbook of social psychology*. Reading, Mass.: Addison-Wesley, 1968.

Anderson, L. F. Variability in the unidimensionality of legislative voting, *Journal of politics*, 26, 1964, 568–585.

Anderson, L. F., Watts, M. W., and Wilcox, A. R. *Legislative roll-call analysis*. Evanston: Northwestern University Press, 1966.

Aristotle. *Posterior analytics*, H. Tredennick, trans. Cambridge: Harvard University Press, 1960.

Bailey, S. K. *Congress makes a law*. New York: Vintage Books, 1950.

Balderston, F. E., and Hoggat, A. C. *Simulation of market processes*. Berkeley: University of California, Institute of Business and Economic Research, 1962.

Barber, J. D. Social interaction among town boards of finance. Paper presented at the 1964 meeting of the American Political Science Association.

Bauer, R. A., Pool, I., and Dexter, L. A. *American business and public policy*. New York: Atherton Press, 1964.

Belknap, G. M. A method for analyzing legislative behavior, *Midwest journal of politics*, 2, 1958, 377–402.

Berger, J., Cohen, B. P., Snell, J. O., and Zelditch, M. *Types of formalization in small group research*. Boston: Houghton Mifflin, 1962.

Blalock, H. *Causal inferences in nonexperimental research*. Chapel Hill: The University of North Carolina Press, 1964.

Bonini, C. P. *Simulation of information and decision systems in the firm*. Englewood Cliffs: Prentice-Hall, 1963.

Braithwaite, R. B. Models in the empirical sciences. In E. Nagel, P. Suppes, and A. Tarski, eds., *Logic methodology and philosophy of science*. Stanford: Stanford University Press, 1962.

Brimhall, D. R., and Otis, A. S. Consistency of voting in our congressmen, *Journal of applied psychology*, 32, 1948, 1–14.

Brodbeck, M. Models, meanings and theories. In L. Gross, ed., *Symposium on sociological theory*. Evanston: Row Peterson, 1959.

Browning, R. P. Computer programs as theories of political processes, *Journal of politics*, 24, 1962, 562–582.

Campbell, A., Converse, P. E., Miller, W. E., and Stokes, D. E. *The American voter*. New York: Wiley, 1960.

Campbell, D. T., and Fiske, D. W. Convergent and discriminant validation by the multi-trait-multimethod matrix, *Psychological bulletin*, 56, 1959, 81–105.

Carlson, H. B., and Harrell, W. Voting groups among leading congressmen obtained by means of the inverted factor technique, *Journal of social psychology*, 16, 1942, 51–61.

Chapanis, A. Men, machines, and models, *American psychologist*, 16, 1961, 113–131.

Chorufas, D. N. *Systems and simulations.* New York: The Academic Press, 1964.

Clarkson, G. P. *Portfolio selection: A simulation of trust investment.* Englewood Cliffs: Prentice-Hall, 1962.

Clarkson, G. P., and Simon, H. A. Simulation of individual and group behavior, *American economic review*, 50, 1960, 920–932.

Clausen, A. R. The measurement of legislative group behavior, *Midwest journal of politics*, no. 2, 1967, 212–225.

Cnudde, C. F., and McCrone, D. J. The linkage between constituency attitudes and congressional voting behavior: a causal model, *American political science review*, 60, 1966, 66–73.

Coe, R. M. Conflict, interference and aggression: a computer simulation, *Behavioral science*, 9, 1964, 186–197.

Cohen, K. J. *Computer simulation of the shoe, leather, hide sequence.* Englewood Cliffs: Prentice-Hall, 1960.

Cohen, K. J., and Cyert, R. M. Simulation of organizational behavior. In J. G. March, ed., *Handbook of organizations.* Chicago: Rand McNally, 1965.

Colby, K. M. Computer simulation of a neurotic process. In S. Tomkins and S. Messick, eds., *Computer simulation of personality.* New York: Wiley, 1963.

Colby, K. M., and Gilbert, J. P. Programming a computer model of neurosis, *Journal of mathematical psychology*, 1, 1964, 405–417.

Coleman, J. S. Mathematical models and computer simulations. In L. Faris, ed., *Handbook of modern sociology.* Chicago: Rand McNally, 1963.

Coleman, J. S. Analysis of social structures and simulation of social processes with an electronic computer, *Educational and psychological measurement*, 21, 1961, 203–218.

Coleman, J. S., and Waldorf, F. Study of a voting system with computer techniques. Baltimore: Johns Hopkins University, 1962, mimeo.

Committee on Political Parties of the American Political Science Association. *Toward a more responsible two-party system.* New York: Rinehart, 1950.

Converse, P. E. Information flow and the stability of partisan attitudes, *Public opinion quarterly*, 26, 1962, 578–600.

Crane, W., Jr. A caveat on roll-call studies of party voting, *Midwest journal of political science*, 4, 1960, 237–249.

Crane, W., Jr. Do representatives represent?, *Journal of politics*, 22, 1960a, 245–249.

Cyert, R. M., and March, J. G. *A behavioral theory of the firm*. Englewood Cliffs: Prentice-Hall, 1963.

Dahl, R. A. *Congress and foreign policy*. New York: Harcourt, Brace, & World, 1950.

Dawson, R. E. Simulation in the social sciences. In H. Guetzkow, ed., *Simulation in social science: readings*. Englewood Cliffs: Prentice-Hall, 1962.

Deutsch, K. W., Singer, J. D., and Smith, K. The organizing efficiency of theories, *American behavioral scientist*, 9, 1965, 30–33.

Dexter, L. A. The representative and his district. In R. L. Peabody, and N. Polsby, eds., *New perspectives on the house of representatives*. Chicago: Rand McNally, 1965.

Dye, T. R. A comparison of constituency influences in the upper and lower chambers of a state legislature, *Western political quarterly*, 14, 1961, 473–481.

Eulau, H., and Hinckley, K. Legislative institutions and processes. In James A. Robinson, ed., *Political science annual 1966*. Indianapolis: Bobbs-Merrill, 1966.

Eysenck, H. J. *The Psychology of Politics*. London: Routledge, 1954.

Farnsworth, D. N. A comparison of the senate and its foreign relations committee, *Western political quarterly*, 14, 1961, 168–175.

Farris, C. D. A method for determining ideological groupings in the congress. *Journal of politics*, 20, 1958, 308–338.

Fattu, N. A. An introduction to simulation. In N. A. Fattu and S. Elam, eds., *Simulation models for education*. Bloomington, Ind.: Phi Delta Kappa, 1965.

Feigenbaum, E. A. The simulation of verbal learning behavior, *Proceedings of the western joint computer conference*, 19, 1961, 121–132.

Feigenbaum, E. A. The simulation of verbal learning behavior. In E. A. Feigenbaum and J. Feldman, eds., *Computers and thought*. New York: McGraw-Hill, 1963.

Feldman, J. Simulation of behavior in a binary choice experiment. In E. A. Feigenbaum and J. Feldman, eds., *Computers and thought*. New York: McGraw-Hill, 1963.

Fenno, R. F., Jr. The house appropriations committee as a political system: the problem of integration, *American political science review*, 56, 1962, 310–325.

Fiellin, A. The functions of informal groups: a state delegation. In R. L. Peabody and N. W. Polsby, eds., *New perspectives on the house of representatives*. Chicago: Rand McNally, 1963.

Fiellin, A. The function of informal groups in legislative institutions: a case study, *Journal of politics*, 24, 1962, 72–91.

Fisher, S., and Lubin, A. Distance as a determinant of influence in a two-person serial interaction situation, *Journal of abnormal and social psychology*, 56, 1958, 230–238.

Francis, W. L. Influence and interaction in a state legislative body, *American political science review*, 56, 1962, 953–961.

Froman, L. A., Jr. *Congressmen and their constituencies*. Chicago: Rand McNally, 1963.

Froman, L. A., Jr. The importance of individuality in voting in congress, *Journal of politics*, 25, 1963a, 324–332.

Froman, L. A., Jr. Inter-party constituency differences and congressional voting behavior, *American political science review*, 57, 1963b, 57–61.

Froman, L. A., Jr., and Ripley, R. B. Conditions for party leadership: the case of the house democrats, *American political science review*, 59, 1965, 52–63.

Garceau, O., and Silverman, C. A pressure group and the pressured: a case report, *American political science review*, 48, 1954, 672–691.

Geisler, M. The simulation of large-scale military activity, *Management science*, 5, 1959, 359–368.

Gleeck, L. G. 96 congressmen make up their minds, *Public opinion quarterly*, 4, 1940, 3–24.

Goldberg, S. C. Three situational determinants of conformity to social norms, *Journal of abnormal and social psychology*, 59, 1954, 325–329.

Grassmuck, G. *Sectional biases in congress on foreign policy*. Baltimore: Johns Hopkins Press, 1951.

Greenstein, F. I., and Jackson, E. F. A second look at the validity of roll-call analysis, *Midwest journal of political science*, 7, 1963, 156–166.

Guetzkow, H., et al. *Simulation in international relations: developments for research and teaching*. Englewood Cliffs: Prentice-Hall, 1963.

Guetzkow, H., ed. *Simulation in social science: readings*. Englewood Cliffs: Prentice-Hall, 1962.

Guetzkow, H., and Bowes, A. The development of organizations in a laboratory, *Management science*, 3, 1957, 380–402.

Guetzkow, H. The use of simulation in the study of international relations, *Behavioral science*, 4, 1959, 183–191.

Gullahorn, J. T., and Gullahorn, J. E. A computer model of elementary social behavior, *Behavioral science*, 8, 1963, 354–362.

Gullahorn, J. T., and Gullahorn, J. E. Some computer applications in social science, *American sociological review*, 30, 1965, 353–365.

Guttman, L. The basis for scalogram analysis. In S. A. Stouffer, ed., *Measurement and prediction*. Princeton: Princeton University Press, 1950.

Hare, A. P. Computer simulation of interaction in small groups, *Behavioral science*, 6, 1961, 261–265.

Havens, M. C. Metropolitan areas and congress: foreign policy and national security, *Journal of politics*, 26, 1964, 758–774.

Hermann, C. F. Validation problems in games and simulations with special reference to models of international politics, *Behavioral science*, 12, 1967, 216–231.

Hermann, C. F., and Hermann, M. G. An attempt to simulate the outbreak of world war I, *American political science review*, 61, no. 2, 1967, 400–417.

Herniter, J. D. Mathematical design of marketing systems. In J. Beshers, ed., *Computer methods in the analysis of large scale social systems*. Cambridge: Joint Center for Urban Studies, MIT and Harvard, 1965.

Hovland, C., Harvey, O. J., and Sherif, M. Assimilation and contrast effects in reactions to communication and attitude change, *Journal of abnormal and social psychology*, 55, 1957, 244–252.

Hovland, C., and Pritzker, H. A. Extent of opinion change as a function of amount of change advocated, *Journal of abnormal and social psychology*, 54, 1957, 257–261.

Hunt, E. B., and Hovland, C. Programming a model of human concept formation, *Proceedings of the western joint computer conference*, 19, 1961, 145–155.

Huntington, S. P. A revised theory of american party politics. *American political science review*, 44, 1950, 669–677.

Jewell, M. E. Evaluating the decline of southern internationalism through senatorial roll-call votes, *Journal of politics*, 21, 1959, 624–646.

Kaplan, A. *The conduct of inquiry: methodology for behavioral science*. San Francisco: Chandler, 1964.

Keefe, W. Comparative study of the role of political parties in state legislatures, *Western political quarterly*, 9, 1956, 726–742.

Keefe, W. Party government and lawmaking in illinois general assembly, *Northwestern university law review*, 47, 1952, 55–71.

Kessel, J. H. The washington congressional delegation, *Midwest journal of political science*, 8, 1964, 1–21.

Kesselman, M. Presidential leadership in congress on foreign policy, *Midwest journal of political science*, 5, 1961, 284–289.

Key, V. O., Jr. *Southern politics*. New York: Knopf, 1949.

Klahr, D. A computer simulation of the paradox of voting, *American political science review*, 60, no. 2, 1966, 384–391.

Kress, P. F. On validating simulation: with special attention to simulation of international politics. Evanston: Northwestern University, 1966, mimeo.

Lane, R. E. *Political life*. New York: Free Press, 1965.

Lazarsfeld, P. F., Berelson, B. R., and Gaudet, H. *The people's choice*. New York: Columbia University Press, 1948.

Lazarsfeld, P. F., Berelson, B. R., and McPhee, W. N. *Voting*. Chicago: University of Chicago Press, 1954.

Lerche, C. O. *The uncertain south: its changing patterns of politics in foreign policy*. Chicago: Quadrangle Books, 1964.

Loehlin, J. C. A computer program that simulates personality. In S. Tomkins and S. Messick, eds., *Computer simulation of personality*. New York: Wiley, 1963.

Loehlin, J. C. Interpersonal experiments with a computer model of personality, *Journal of personality and social psychology*, 2, 1965, 580–584.

Lowell, A. L. The influence of party upon legislation in england and america, *Annual report of the american historical association*, 1, 1901, 321–343.

McPhee, W. N. Note on a campaign simulator, *Public opinion quarterly*, 25, 1961, 184–193.

McPhee, W. N. Note on a campaign simulator. In W. N. McPhee, ed., *Formal theories of mass behavior*. London: Free Press of Glencoe, 1963.

MacRae, D., Jr. The relation between roll-call votes and constituencies in the massachusetts house of representatives, *American political science review*, 46, 1952, 1046–1055.

MacRae, D., Jr. *Dimensions of congressional voting*. Berkeley and Los Angeles: University of California Press, 1958.

MacRae, D., Jr. Some underlying variables in legislative roll-call votes, *Public opinion quarterly*, 18, 1954, 191–196.

MacRae, D., Jr. Roll-call votes and leadership, *Public opinion quarterly*, 20, 1956, 543–558.

Martin, R. C. *The cities and the federal system.* New York: Atherton, 1965.

Marwell, Gerald. Party, region and the dimensions of conflict in the house of representatives, 1949–1954, *American political science review*, 61, no. 2, 1967, 380–400.

Matthews, D. R. *U. S. senators and their world.* Chapel Hill: University of North Carolina Press, 1960.

Mayhew, D. R. *Party loyalty among congressmen: the difference between democrats and republicans, 1947–1962.* Cambridge: Harvard University Press, 1966.

Meller, N. Legislative behavior research, *Western political quarterly*, 13, 1959, 131–154.

Meller, N. Legislative behavior research revisited: a review of five years of publications, *Western political quarterly*, 18, 1965, 776–793.

Miller, W. E. Majority rule and the representative system. Paper delivered at the American Political Science Association Convention, Washington, D. C., Sept., 1962, as reported in Froman, 1963, p. 117.

Miller, W. E., and Stokes, D. E. Constituency influence in congress, *American political science review*, 57, 1963, 45–56.

Munger, F. J., and Fenno, R. F., Jr. *National politics and federal aid to education.* Syracuse: Syracuse University Press, 1962.

Munitz, M. F. *Space, time and creation.* New York: Collier, 1957.

Naylor, T. H., Balintfy, J. L., Burdick, D. S., and Chu, Kong. *Computer simulation techniques.* New York: Wiley, 1966.

Neustadt, R. E. Presidency and legislation: planning the president's program, *American political science review*, 49, 1955, 980–1021.

Newcomb, T. M., Turner, R. H., and Converse, P. E. *Social psychology.* New York: Holt, Rinehart and Winston, 1965.

Newell, A., Shaw, J. C., and Simon, H. A. Elements of a theory of problem solving, *Psychological review*, 65, 1958, 151–166.

Newell, A., and Simon, H. A. GPS, a program that simulates human thought. In E. A. Feigenbaum and J. Feldman, eds., *Computers and thought.* New York: McGraw-Hill, 1963.

Orcutt, G. H. Simulation of economic systems, *American economic review*, 50, 1960, 893–907.

Orcutt, G. H. Simulation of economic systems. In H. Guetzkow, ed., *Simulation in social science: readings.* Englewood Cliffs: Prentice-Hall, 1962.

Orcutt, G. H., Greenberger, M., Korbel, J., and Rivlin, A. H. *Microanalysis of socioeconomic systems: a simulation study.* New York: Harpers, 1961.

Ozkaptan, H., and Gettig, R. Computer simulation of man-integrated systems, *Behavioral science*, 8, 1963, 259–266.

Parsons, M. B. Quasi-partisan conflict in a one party legislative system: the florida senate, 1947–61, *American political science review*, 56, 1962, 605–615.

Patterson, S. C. Patterns of interpersonal relations in a state legislative group: the wisconsin assembly. *Public opinion quarterly*, 23, 1959, 101–109.

Patterson, S. C. The role of the deviant in the state legislative system: the wisconsin assembly, *Western political quarterly*, 14, 1961, 460–472.

Patterson, S. C. Dimensions of voting in a one-party state legislature, *Public opinion quarterly*, 26, 1962, 185–200.

Pennock, J. R. Party and constituency in postwar agricultural price-support legislation, *Journal of politics*, 18, 1956, 167–210.

Polsby, N. W. Two strategies of influence: choosing a majority leader, 1962. In R. L. Peabody and N. W. Polsby, eds., *New perspectives on the house of representatives.* Chicago: Rand McNally, 1963.

Pool, I., Abelson, R. P., and Popkin, S. *Candidates, strategies, and issues: a computer simulation of the 1960 and 1964 presidential elections.* Cambridge: MIT Press, 1965.

Rapoport, A. *Strategy and conscience.* New York: Harper and Row, 1964.

Rice, S. A. The behavior of legislative groups, *Political science quarterly*, 40, 1925, 60–72.

Rieselbach, L. N. The demography of the congressional vote on foreign aid 1939–1958, *American political science review*, 58, 1964, 577–589.

Rieselbach, L. N. Foreign policy ideology in the eighty-eighth congress: constituency and other correlates. A paper delivered at the annual meeting of the Midwest Conference of Political Scientists, Chicago, April, 1966a.

Rieselbach, L. N. *The roots of isolationism.* Indianapolis: Bobbs-Merrill, 1966.

Ripley, R. B. The party whip organizations in the United States House of Representatives, *American political science review*, 58, 1964, 561–576.

Ritti, R. P., and Fair, C. P. Simulating the behavioral consequences of changes in organizational systems. Paper delivered at the American Sociological Association Convention, Chicago, Sept., 1965.

Roach, H. G. Sectionalism in congress (1870–1890), *American political science review*, 19, 1925, 500–526.

Robinson, J. A. *Congress and foreign policy.* Homewood, Ill.: Dorsey Press, 1962.

Rokkan, S. The comparative study of political participation: notes toward a perspective on current research. In A. Ranney, ed., *Essays on the behavioral study of politics.* Urbana: University of Illinois Press, 1962.

Rosenberg, M. J., and Abelson, R. P. An analysis of cognitive balance. In M. J. Rosenberg, *et al., Attitude organization and change.* New Haven: Yale Press, 1960.

Ross, M. H. Some correlates of voting support for the leadership in the house of representatives. First year paper submitted to the Department of Political Science, Northwestern University, July, 1965.

Routt, G. C. Interpersonal relationships and the legislative process, *Annals of the american academy of political and social science*, 195, 1938, 129–136.

Rummel, R. J. Dimensions of conflict behavior within and between nations, *General systems yearbook*, 8, 1963, 1–49.

Rustow, D. A. The politics of compromise: a study of parties and cabinet governments in sweden. Princeton: Princeton University Press, 1955.

Shubik, M. Simulation of the industry and the firm, *American economic review*, 50, 1960, 907–919.

Silverman, C. The legislator's view of the legislative process, *Public opinion quarterly*, 18, 1954, 180–190.

Simon, H. A., and Newell, A. Models: their uses and limitations. In L. White, ed., *The state of the social sciences.* Chicago: University of Chicago Press, 1956.

Snyder, R. C. Some perspectives on the use of experimental techniques in the study of international relations. In H. Guetzkow, *et al., Simulation in international relations: developments for research and teaching.* Englewood Cliffs: Prentice-Hall, 1963.

Sorauf, F. J. *Party and representation.* New York: Atherton Press, 1962.

Starbuck, W. Testing case-descriptive models, *Behavioral science*, 6, 1961, 191–200.

Tanter, R. Dimensions of conflict behavior within and between nations, 1958–1960. Ph. D. dissertation, Department of Government, Indiana University, August, 1964.

Truman, D. B. *The congressional party.* New York: Wiley, 1959.

Truman, D. B. The state delegations and the structure of party voting in the united states house of representatives, *American political science review*, 50, 1956, 1023–1045.

Turner, J. *Party and constituency: pressures on congress.* Baltimore: Johns Hopkins Press, 1951.

Turner, J. Responsible parties: a dissent from the floor, *American political science review*, 45, 1951a, 143–153.

Wahlke, J. C. Behavioral analyses of representative bodies. A. Ranney, ed., *Essays on the behavioral study of politics.* Urbana: University of Illinois Press, 1962.

Wahlke, J. C., Eulau, H., Buchanan, W., and Ferguson, L. C. *The legislative system: explorations in legislative behavior.* New York: Wiley, 1962.

Westerfield, H. B. *Foreign policy and party politics.* New Haven: Yale University Press, 1955.

Zimbardo, P. G. Involvement, communication discrepancy, and conformity, *Journal of abnormal and social psychology*, 60, 1960, 86–94.

Index of Subjects

Index of Names